SERVICE-LEARNING IN ASIA

To: Prof. Yates

With friendship and appreciation.

— Jun
09/20/0

SERVICE-LEARNING IN ASIA
CURRICULAR MODELS AND PRACTICES

EDITED BY
JUN XING AND
CAROL HOK KA MA

香港大學出版社
HONG KONG UNIVERSITY PRESS

Hong Kong University Press
14/F Hing Wai Centre
7 Tin Wan Praya Road
Aberdeen
Hong Kong

© Hong Kong University Press 2010

Hardback   ISBN 978-988-8028-46-7
Paperback   ISBN 978-988-8028-47-4

British Library Cataloguing-in-Publication Data
A catalogue copy for this book is available from the British Library

Secure On-line Ordering
http://www.hkupress.org

Printed and bound by Goodrich International Printing Co. Ltd., Hong Kong, China

Contents

Foreword

Service-learning, especially in the United States, has a long history as part of the school and university curriculum. But service-learning is a relatively new concept in Asia. There still exist some misconceptions and misunderstanding of what service-learning is and how it should be implemented. I am very pleased to see the publication of this important volume on service-learning in Asia, providing some conceptual framework and many interesting case studies. This volume will certainly become a major reference for studies in service-learning in the region.

First, service-learning is not simply voluntary work or community service that each student has to undertake for a certain number of hours a year as required by the university. It should actually be integrated into and enhance the curriculum. It is usually credit-bearing and for partial fulfillment of the requirements of an academic subject. The service rendered is through structured preparation, supervision and reflection. Second, service-learning should involve university-wide participation and should not be applicable only to some departments such as social work, social sciences, and humanities. Medical, business and sciences students, for example, can easily incorporate service-learning into their academic studies. Third, the assessment of service-learning undertaken by a student should not be based only on the outcome of services provided but also on the processes gone through by the student. Fourth, service-learning should be distinguished from internship which emphasizes skill and professional training and takes largely private interests into account. Service-learning emphasizes experiential learning and takes largely public interest into account.

The purpose of service-learning is learning how to serve the community better and at the same time learning better an academic subject through providing services to the community. Service-learning is important in enhancing academic learning as well as character forming in liberal education.

There is no one single formula for implementing service-learning, which is to a large extent culture, location, and institution specific, though we can develop a common framework and a generally accepted conceptualization. This volume has collected a number of excellent papers on service-learning with reference to the region as a whole and to particular Asian countries and territories. It will fill in the gap now existing in the literature on service-learning in Asia. In the past few years, higher education in the region has increasingly given attention to service-learning; many conferences have been held and many universities have introduced it to their academic curricula. It is not always easy to establish and implement successfully service-learning in a university. First of all, a strong support and commitment of the senior management (especially the president) is required. Second, though it is not essential and possible that all faculty members would participate, a university-wide endorsement with reference to mission and vision is important. Third, students, faculty and staff who participate must be strongly motivated and not half-hearted. Fourth, a dedicated service-learning office must be set up for the complex work of promotion, liaising, co-ordination, matching, training, monitoring, and research. Fifth, adequate funding for service-learning in an institution, preferably a sizable earmarked grant or donation, would be essential for long-term planning and development purposes. Lastly, a good network for establishing international and local partnerships is needed for finding suitable organizations to host the students.

As a former president of Lingnan University who initiated service-learning in the university and set up the first dedicated service-learning office in Hong Kong, I warmly welcome the publication of this collection. I have faith in the success and rapid development of service-learning in Asia.

Edward K. Y. Chen
Distinguished Fellow, Centre of Asian Studies, The University of Hong Kong
Former President, Lingnan University (1995–2007)

November 2009

Contributors

J. CHITHRA has been a senior professor of mathematics at Lady Doak College, Madurai, India since 1987. She obtained her master of arts in mathematics and philosophy from Madras Christian College, affiliated to Madras University, with a specialization in cryptography. She is currently a coordinator of the Centre for Outreach and Service-Learning Program at the college. She has been a program officer of the National Service Scheme in the college for 6 years and has been coordinating all the extension programs of the college for the past 8 years. She has attended conferences and workshops and presented papers on service-learning at national and international levels. She has also attended the Inter-Cultural Course on Women and Society at Manila in the Philippines and is actively involved in women's studies at the college.

Helen Mary JACQUELINE is a senior lecturer in economics at Lady Doak College, Madurai, India. She is currently a coordinator for the Centre for Outreach and Service-Learning Program at the college. She obtained five postgraduate degrees: an MA in economics from Madurai Kamaraj University, Madurai; an MA in population studies from Annamalai University, Chidambaram; a master of philosophy (MPhil) in applied economics from Jawaharlal Nehru University, New Delhi; a master of human resource management (MHRM) from Annamalai University, Chidambaram; and a master of business administration (MBA) from Annamali University, Chidambaram. She was the program officer of the National Service Scheme for 5 years and is actively involved in service-learning program and human rights activities. She has published more than 10 articles and presented papers in about 18 seminars and conferences at state, regional, national and international levels.

Kwok Hung LAI, PhD, is a senior student affairs officer at the Hong Kong Institute of Education. He is currently the director of the Institute of Student Affairs of the Asia-Pacific Student Services Association, after serving as treasurer since 2002. He is also the vice-chairman of the Hong Kong Student Services Association. Dr Lai is a registered social worker with over 26 years of professional experiences in working with youths in the fields of social work and education. He has published more than 50 articles in local newspapers and international journals. His research interests are in youth work, crime and delinquency, civic education, campus culture, student learning, and career aspirations.

Dennis LEE is regional vice president and managing director, Asia, for Students in Free Enterprise (SIFE), a global non-profit organization represented in 48 countries. Previously, he was deputy executive director at Singapore International Foundation (SIF). Academically, Mr Lee holds three postgraduate degrees: an MBA from the University of Hull, United Kingdom; a master of divinity (MDiv); and a master of theological studies (MTS) from Regent College, Vancouver, Canada. He also obtained a postgraduate diploma in business administration from the Society of Business Practitioners, United Kingdom. His professional and tertiary education in marketing and civil engineering led to diplomas in these disciplines from the Chartered Institute of Marketing, United Kingdom, and the Singapore Polytechnic respectively.

Carol Hok Ka MA, PhD, is assistant director of the Office of Service-Learning and an adjunct assistant professor in the Department of Sociology and Social Policy at Lingnan University. She was awarded a W. T. Chan Fellowship to study and practice service-learning (elderly-related programs) at the University of California, Los Angeles. She was also awarded a Lingnan Foundation Scholarship to do a service-learning research internship on the topic of "doctor-older patient relationship through negotiation" at the National Primary Health Care Centre, the University of Manchester. Currently, she serves on several important government committees in Hong Kong, including the Hong Kong Awards for Young People; Commission on Youth; Working Group on Active Ageing, Elderly Commission; Tuen Mun District Coordinating Committee on Promotion of Volunteer Service, Social Welfare Department; Fight Crime Committee (Tuen Mun District), Home Affairs Department; and as school governor for Lingnan Dr Chung Wing Kwong Memorial Secondary School. Her rich experiences in service-learning inspire her to explore different teaching/learning models/pedagogies in the Asia-Pacific Region.

Charn MAYOT is director of St. Martin Center for Professional Ethics and Service Learning, Student Affairs, Assumption University, Thailand. He has been in charge of teaching business and professional ethics seminar and supervising a service-learning program for undergraduate students at Assumption University since 1998. He is also an ethics trainer for administrators of some corporations in his country. He has written a number of articles in the areas of applied ethics, moral education, moral development, and service-learning. He was formerly a lecturer of applied ethics at the Graduate School of Philosophy and Religions at Assumption University. He used to collaborate with UNESCO to organize projects and promote peace and harmony in six countries in the Mekhong River Basin region between 2001 and 2005.

Florence MCCARTHY is vice president for Asian affairs at International Partnership for Service-Learning and Leadership (IPSL). She received her PhD in sociology and MA in sociology/anthropology from Michigan State University; and BA in history/political science from the University of California, Berkeley. She is a visiting professor at International Christian University (ICU), Tokyo, Japan. Past positions include: associate professor and director of International Education Development, Teachers College, Columbia University; senior lecturer, College of Human Ecology, Cornell University; advisor, Head Women's Section, Ministry of Agriculture, Bangladesh; and Policy and Program Development, Norwegian Overseas Research and Development, Oslo, Norway. She has been awarded grants from Fulbright, the National Institute of Health, and the Norwegian government.

Jens MUELLER is an associate professor for entrepreneurship and strategy at Waikato Management School, New Zealand. He also serves as editor for the *Journal of Asia Entrepreneurship and Sustainability* and *International Journal of Indigenous Entrepreneurship, Strategy, Advancement and Education*. He is the foundation chairman of the International Quality Education Foundation (IQEF). Previously, he served as regional vice president and managing director, Asia, Students in Free Enterprise (SIFE).

Mutsuko MURAKAMI is a service-learning program instructor at the International Christian University. She obtained her BA from Tokyo's Sophia University and master of science in journalism (MSJ) from the Graduate School of Journalism of Columbia University, New York City. She worked in journalism for many years, primarily as staff correspondent for *Asiaweek* magazine (a subsidary of Time Inc.). She started teaching journalism and communication at Sophia in 1993 and later service-learning courses while acting as the program coordinator at ICU. She is currently teaching service-learning related courses at ICU.

Takashi NISHIO is a professor of public policy and administration, and dean of the College of Liberal Arts (since April 2009), International Christian University. He served as director of the Service Learning Center of ICU from 2005 to 2007.

Enrique G. ORACION holds BA and MA degrees in sociology from Silliman University, Dumaguete City, Philippines and a PhD in anthropology from the University of San Carlos, Cebu City, the Philippines. He is a full professor at Silliman University and teaches in the Department of Sociology and Anthropology, College of Arts and Sciences; School of Public Affairs and Governance; and College of Education. He is also the current director of the Research and Development Center of Silliman University. His particular research interests include the human dimensions of natural resources management and governance, children and gender issues, the anthropology of tourism, and service-learning.

Jane Szutu PERMAUL, EdD, a lifetime student of higher education focused on student and organizational development, introduced service-learning to the University of California, Los Angeles (UCLA) and nationally worked with other service-learning pioneers in exploring the challenges of integrating community service with academic learning as part of higher education, beginning in the late 1960s to today. Emigrating from China to the United States, Dr Perumal received her BA in economics from Oberlin College in Ohio, master of science (MS) in student affairs administration from Southern Illinois University, and EdD in higher education from UCLA. Her interests in service-learning and cross-cultural learning continue through her capacity as assistant vice chancellor of student affairs, emeritus and adjunct professor of education at UCLA, and as a trustee of the Lingnan Foundation.

John H. POWERS is a professor of communication studies at Hong Kong Baptist University (HKBU). He served as director of the Service-Learning Program there for nearly 5 years. His research interests include communication in Chinese communities, communication theory, and public communication. Before coming to HKBU in 1993, he taught at Texas A&M University in the United States for 16 years. His books include *Public Speaking: The Lively Art* (1994), *Civic Discourse, Civil Society, and Chinese Communities* (1999), and *The Social Construction of SARS* (2008).

Yutaka SATO is a professor of Japanese linguistics and director of the Japanese Language Programs at the International Christian University (ICU), Tokyo, Japan. He received his PhD in linguistics from the University of Hawaii at Manoa. He served as director of the Service Learning Center at ICU from 2007 to 2009.

Jun XING is a professor and chair of ethnic studies at Oregon State University. He is the author/editor of six other books, including *Baptized in the Fire of Revolution, The American Social Gospel and the YMCA in China: 1919–1937* (1996), *Asian America through the Lens: History, Representations and Identity* (1998), *Reversing the Lens: Ethnicity, Race, Gender and Sexuality through Film* (2003), *Teaching for Change: The Difference, Power and Discrimination Model* (2006), and *Seeing Color: Indigenous Peoples and Racialized Ethnic Minorities in Oregon* (2007).

Kano YAMAMOTO is managing trustee of International Christian University, Tokyo, Japan. He served as an economist at the Bank of Japan, International Monetary Fund, comptroller of UNICEF, and professor at International Christian University. He was the first director of ICU Service Learning Center and currently serves as its advisor.

Bai-Chuan YANG is an associate professor, dean of the Office of Student Affairs at Fu Jen Catholic University, and deputy chief executive secretary of the Academic Association of Chinese Student Affairs. He received his MBA degree from Virginia Polytechnic Institute and State University (1989) and PhD in business administration from Fu Jen Catholic University (2006). His current research mainly focuses on core competence, service-learning, and business ethics. He also served as a business consultant for Mon-Ya Management Consulting Firm.

Jen-Chi YEN is director of the Service-Learning Center and the Jesuit Mission Office at Fu Jen Catholic University. Father David received his MA in mass communication from Loyola Marymount University. He served as chairman of the Kuangchi Program Service, and on the evaluation committee of the Golden Horse and Golden Bell Awards. He is also the producer of various TV programs and writes movie reviews.

Introduction: Service-learning in Asia

Jun Xing and Carol Hok Ka Ma

Four years ago in 2006, when Jun was working for the United Board of Christian Higher Education in Asia (United Board), he visited International Christian University (ICU) in Tokyo, where he learned about the inspiring story of an ICU-NJU (Nanjing University) service-learning project. In January of 2005, a group of ICU students went to Nanjing University and participated in a service-learning program, sponsored by the Amity Foundation, where ICU and NJU students jointly produced a new play called *Zouba!* (Let's Go). The play portrays a group of students from Japan and China, trying courageously to move beyond history and start a painful, but meaningful journey of reconciliation. Despite its high political risks and initial tension, the joint performance in both Tokyo and Nanjing in the following year turned out to be a resounding success and made a huge splash in the news media. Here is a quote from a Japanese student participant reported on NPR's "Morning Edition," on January 27, 2007:

> "That first night we all went to dinner," she (Michiyo Oi, who wrote much of the script) recalls. "We sat around talking, and I figured they must be wondering what we were thinking. Each of us introduced ourselves, and when my turn came, I started to talk about the war, about what a shame it was that we did such terrible things. The air froze. Until then we were all laughing. The moment I mentioned the war, everyone went pale. The Chinese students looked at me as if they couldn't believe the way I'd brought this up."

As we all know, because of historical reasons, Chinese and Japanese are very much divided about that particular period of history. The Nanjing massacre, or what the late historian Iris Chang called the "Rape of Nanjing," has been a focal point of contention between these two countries. It has become a taboo topic for politicians and diplomats from both sides. It was the service-learning project that brought students together and the joint theatrical production became the ice-breaker that allowed students to openly share their emotions and exchange ideas. It was such a powerful and profound learning experience for both the Chinese and Japanese students that the ICU Foundation in New York is planning to make a documentary about the student experience.

Having invested his life in cross-cultural and international studies for over two decades, Jun was greatly inspired by the story and just witnessed the tremendous potential of international service-learning at its best. Indeed, connecting academic study with community service through structured reflection, service-learning is now widely recognized in the world as a movement that is transforming education. As an instructional philosophy and pedagogy, service-learning has become a major force in Asia. Between 2006 and 2007, on behalf of the United Board Jun traveled to over a dozen university campuses in several countries and witnessed how service-learning was recognized and celebrated for its pedagogical values across the region.

Indeed, many leading universities and colleges across Asia had established service-learning centers or programs, supporting a dedicated core of faculty and serving an increasingly larger student population. Lingnan University, for example, was the first to set up the Office of Service-Learning (OSL) on campus. Clearly echoing Lingnan's long-standing motto "Education for Service," OSL is devoted to fostering student-centered learning and whole-person development model.[1] Between 2006 and 2009, over 1,000 Lingnan students from various disciplines, such as social sciences, business and arts have participated in the three core programs in service-learning, including the Lingnan Healthcare Program (LHCP), the Lingnan Community Care Program (LCCP), and the Lingnan Service-Learning Evaluation Program (LS-LEP). These participants were required to fulfill a service-learning practicum with at least 30 hours of service and complete a subject-related project in a semester. So far Lingnan students have served over 100 organizations (government, non-profit, schools, and corporate firms) and registered 70,000 service hours for the needy, elderly, youth, patients, and single-parent families. In addition, over 80 students have joined international service-learning programs, sponsored by OSL and engaged in service-learning activities in Yunnan, Beijing, Taipei, Guangzhou and several cities in the United States.

For another example, under the auspices of the Singapore International Foundation, over a five-year period (2000–05), the Youth Expedition Project sent over 12,000 students on service-learning assignments across Southeast Asia, China and India.[2] In the meantime, the CBI (community-based instruction) program at Hong Kong Baptist University (HKBU) partnered with 100 local service agencies and conducted several hundred service-learning projects in Hong Kong and elsewhere.[3] What is more, in Taiwan, over half (86 out of 146) of its universities and colleges have incorporated service-learning into their core curriculum.[4] The Ministry of Education in Taipei plans to add service-learning into its annual regular accreditation process. In a sense, service-learning has come of age in Asia and its place in the Asian academy has been secured.

However, despite these accomplishments, there are few scholarly publications on Asian-based practices and contexts of service-learning. Most of the written works on service-learning so far are monographs, teaching anthologies or guidebooks published in the United States, including series and booklets coming from the American Association of Higher Education (AAHE), International Partnership for Service-Learning (IPSL) and Campus Compact. The 21-volume set 'Service-Learning in the Disciplines', published by AAHE, is a good example of this increasing body of literature. Although these are seminal works that have made significant contributions to the development of service-learning in Asia, we see the urgent need of a book that explores specifically local or indigenous practices of service-learning in Asian societies. This anthology is a modest attempt to help fill that gap by focusing on service-learning in the Asian contexts, both reflective of international trends but also distinctive in its own local and regional characteristics, given the tremendous diversity within Asian societies.

As disparate as they may seem in length, cultures (a true mosaic), disciplines (from social work to business) and institutions (public, private or Christian by nature), the essays in the collection coalesce around three major thematic foci and contribute to the overall objectives of the publication together.

Service-learning and Indigenous Cultural Traditions

> Service-learning is not intended to be used in every course, but it is possible to incorporate it into any discipline. It is not possible to design a single model that effectively integrates service-learning into academic study for all disciplines or institutions. Service-learning must be contextualized and relevant to meet unique and evolving needs . . . Thus, service-learning takes different forms in different contexts.[5]

This quote from the authors of Chapter 4 in the volume captures the first reigning theme and objective of the book, that is, promotion of the concept of indigenous or local and culturally specific knowledge or systems of knowledge. Indeed, service-learning, like any learning, is not culture-neutral but deeply imbedded in the historical and social contexts of each educational system. Although service-learning is primarily a Western term, the meaning, understanding and practices vary from society to society. In the Philippines, for example, service-learning is often practiced at colleges and universities that have a Christian tradition, while in India it grows out of a vision of national self-reliance in the post-colonial era. For Hong Kong the development of service-learning has benefited from the government's emphasis on whole-person education. In contemporary China, as some scholars argue, service-learning represents a way of countering the growing individualism and materialism in a rapidly transforming society.

As indicated in the title, cultural diversity and local themes are the defining characteristics of the book. For example, it is refreshing to read Chapter 1, where Charn Mayot provides the national contexts of service-learning in Thailand. He explains that although the very term "service-learning" was not coined until 1967 in the United States and it was not used in Thailand as late as in the early 1990s, social concern has been a part of higher education in the country for a very long time through the concepts of community service and social exposure.[6] Similarly, in Chapter 7, Enrique Oracion helps the readers to distinguish service-learning as a "pro-social behavior, but short of altruism," a time-honored Filipino cultural tradition, "because the latter means helping others without any expectation of return," while service-learning "maybe less or not at all altruistic because of the learning or the grade the students expect to earn in exchange."[7]

Recently, there has been a growing debate over indigenous knowledge and cultural traditions in the academy. The World Indigenous Nations Higher Education Consortium (WINHEC), for example, was established in 2002 by indigenous peoples' representatives from Australia, the United States, Canada, and Norway. WINHEC's goals were to advance indigenous peoples' endeavors in and through higher education and establish an accreditation body for their own higher education institutions and initiatives. In the meantime, international attention has turned to intellectual property laws to preserve, protect, and promote traditional knowledge. In 2005, the South Asian Association for Regional Cooperation (SAARC) sponsored a conference in Delhi, India, and announced the initiative to create a digital library system for classifying the region's traditional knowledge and linking it to the international patent classification system.

The papers collected in the volume demonstrate how students engaged in service-learning can benefit from, and contribute to, the development and promotion of indigenous knowledge and traditions. A good case in point was the Students in Free Enterprise (SIFE) program discussed in Chapter 6, which provided ample evidences of how service-learning students from Singapore worked with the tribal communities in Australia and the indigenous Maori population near Whakatane, New Zealand.[8] Equally telling was the eco-tourism project taken on by Assumption University students in collaboration with several local organizations at Mooban Khanim in Phang Nga Province, Thailand. Mooban Khanim is in the area hit by the tsunami in 2004. Forty faculty and students learned that the village was not destroyed because it was protected by a vast mangrove forest around the village. Community members realized that the mangrove forest was both a source of food and a natural wall that protected the community from strong wind and giant waves. That knowledge from the villagers helped Assumption University faculty and students launch a multi-year service-learning project for the mangrove forest preservation in a sustainable manger.[9]

It is also heartening to learn that in Chiang Mai, Northern Thailand, students of Payap University executed their service-learning projects in the library by digitalizing artifacts, rare books, and audio-video materials on northern Thai culture. They had aptly named the project the "local wisdom initiative," which attempted to preserve and document northern Thai dialects, folk songs, recipes, architectural designs and other cultural relicts. Altogether, they have identified 1,000 photos, 2,000 slides, 60 CDs, 123 video tapes, 244 audio tapes and 50 rare books. Those prized collections will soon be made available for researchers worldwide.[10]

Over recent years, a growing rank of scholars has called for a paradigm shift in liberal arts education. Specifically, they ask for a shift of emphasis upon the transformative rather than only the utilitarian value of knowledge. Indigenous knowledge, the philosophical, literary, scientific knowledge, as part of the cultural heritage and history of the local communities is an important part of that transformative knowledge. Unlike the "objective" or "scientifically based" intellectual paradigms, indigenous knowledge can be experientially learned in the field. Readers will pick up ample examples from this book that service-learning, as a powerful experiential pedagogy, is one of the best pedagogical tools we have to acquire that knowledge.

Service-learning and Social Justice Education

> Injustice anywhere is a threat to justice everywhere. We are caught in an inescapable network of mutuality, tied in a single garment of destiny. Whatever affects one directly, affects all indirectly.[11]

This quote from the late US civil rights activist and leader the Rev. Martin Luther King, Jr. brings to the fore the second theme of the volume: service-learning and the concept of social justice education. Although service-learning has been adopted widely among faculty, administrators and educators, the misconception of service-learning as charity work is still well around and alive. Some faculty and students have expressed their skepticism about service-learning simply because they feel that such endeavors amount to little more than "charity" work or, even worse, "distractions" from core disciplinary competencies.

Indeed, we may have to admit that this "charity" type of service-learning is still employed by some nonprofit organizations, including universities and colleges, and some service-learning projects lack a political awareness component and the service students perform treats social symptoms, without addressing the root causes of the social disparities, poverty conditions and medical maladies. As Kwok Hung Lai writes in Chapter 3, "Learning from serving others is not automatic. Students serving meals to the homeless, mentoring at-risk youth, and visiting chronically ill patients enjoyed the work and felt satisfied from such altruistic experiences, but did not necessarily engage in critical thinking about the existence of poverty, youth policy, and health-care reform. These experiences may even promote a power imbalance of the privileged 'haves' providing for the 'have-nots'."[12]

To help debunk this misperception and realize the full potential of service-learning, service-learning scholars and practitioners are pushing the advocacy and social change agenda. The stories told by faculty and students in this collection provide ample examples about how faculty and students get involved in policy-related learning and community engagement. A good place to start is to teach students about the social construction of human differences and their own unearned privileges. Chapter 7 illustrates vividly how doing service-learning in Filipino rural communities challenged non-Filipino students in the most personal way, "the comfort of air-conditioned bedrooms, the soothing baths with running hot and cold water in clean bathrooms, the savor of favored food at home or in restaurants, and many other privileges in the urban world are temporarily denied to them . . ."[13] While completing their "social exposure" project, a group of Assumption University students, for another example, witnessed the dire situation of street children in Pattaya and reflected on their own unearned privileges. They were "strongly struck by the fact that these children live on 12 baht a day" and that these children had never tasted fruit before. In comparison, a majority of the students themselves go and see a movie several times a week and spent more than 100 baht for each movie.[14] They learned that sacrificing one movie each week could potentially help one child to be fed for seven days. Similarly, a Singaporean student performing service-learning in Lijiang, China, wrote, "We saw ourselves as fortunate and felt the need to contribute to a less privileged society in our own capacity and capability."[15]

For social justice education, some service-learning have introduced Paulo Freire's concept of transformative processes for service-learning operations, which calls for changing public policy as well as creating change agents. As discussed by John H. Powers in Chapter 5, the CBI program at HKBU promotes the concept of problem-based learning, which "was defined as a teaching method that builds the instructional process around one or more complex problems that the course content may be used to solve."[16] The expected learning outcome of the CBI program, according to Powers, is to encourage students to identify real-life problems from the community and apply knowledge they have learned in seeking their solutions.

Doing service-learning in the Philippines taught the International Service-Learning Model Program (ISLMP) students the enormous disparities between the rich and the poor in the country. One ready example, given in Chapter 7, was the student experience of attending a lavish birthday party of a local politician. Despite the festive mood of the party, a female non-Filipino student was saddened by the lavishness, which presented such a powerful contrast to the poverty they saw being experienced by so many in the community day in and day out.[17] These examples clearly demonstrate how direct community engagement helps ISLMP students develop a transformative perspective on the critical issues of social inequality.

Working for peace and reconciliation was another example cited by several authors in service-learning for social justice education. As discussed earlier, after its successful experience for the joint-production of *"Zouba,"* ICU's service-learning office is planning a follow-up reconciliation program in Nanjing in the near future, where ICU students will acknowledge history and take ownership of Japan's war policies. "This may be a rather unusual agenda for service-learning," as the authors write in Chapter 2, "but as nationals of a country that invaded Asian countries and committed atrocities during modern times, creating this understanding is something very important for all Japanese as global citizens."[18]

Nowadays, social justice ideals are broadly embraced by faculty and students, but oftentimes students are exposed to issues of injustice or inequity only as an abstraction. Service-learning offers a proven pedagogy for moving the discussion of human rights and social justice from the classroom to the streets, where it takes on human meaning and the very concept of social justice can be, therefore, translated into passion and commitment for the students.

Service-learning and the Concept of Multicultural Symbiosis[19]

> If you give people fish, they can eat for a day.
> If you teach them how to fish they can eat for a lifetime.
> If you teach them to learn, they don't have to eat fish all their life.[20]

This pithy quote from Chapter 9 captures the spirit of service-learning in promoting cross-cultural and world literacy. Chapters 2 and 7, for example, describe in detail how in 2006 the six cooperative member schools of the Service-Learning Asia Network (SLAN) first introduced the concept of "multicultural symbiosis" or *kyosei* (meaning "living together" in Japanese) as the key learning objective for the International Service-Learning (ISLMP) program.[21]

In ecology, symbiosis, according to Enrique G. Oracion, refers to a mutually beneficial relationship among organisms. "When applied to human interaction amidst cultural diversity," he writes, "the concept of multicultural symbiosis implies how the coming together of people with diverse cultural backgrounds offers relative benefits to all involved."[22] In both Chapters 2 and 7, readers will find very successful cases of ISLMP participants broke down their long-time held stereotypes against local cultures and residents. Living closer to the Filipino communities, for example, they observed that school children came to school late, not because they were lazy, but "because they must walk three to four hours before reaching school" and "some pupils had to cross rivers several times, which made it difficult to go to school during bad weather."[23]

However, to reach this lofty goal of multicultural symbiosis, it takes vision, care and high ethical standards with regard to power, capacity, equity and sustainability. Several chapters in the book shed light on the sticky side of service, the all-important ethical conduct of service-learning in a cross-cultural or international context. Indeed, there are risks or pitfalls of all kinds in conducting service-learning, especially international service-learning. For example, some of us are familiar with the phenomenon of "academic tourism," referring to those short and superficial stunts overseas without clearly defined learning objectives. Occasionally, students have talked about their service-learning class as a glorified vacation or a visit, a sign of the so-called academic tourism.

Furthermore, we may have heard about those "island programs," where students often stick together among themselves with little or no interaction with the local communities. The entire service project could become exploitive of the stakeholders and communities. Worse still, our faculty and students might try to make other people in our own image, or use service as a way of exercising their sense of generosity or beneficence (read paternalism, patronization or "colonial mentality"). Those "benevolent programs" reinforce personal bias and cultural prejudice against other people. The programs immediately become counter-productive and destructive.

In view of all these potential problems, as service-learning faculty and scholars, how do we set up some useful parameters or criteria for the ethical conduct of service-learning? Reading through the volume, readers will find four broadly defined themes emerge from the pages, namely power-related issues, capacity-related issues, equity-related issues and sustainability-related issues.

For power-related issues, service-learning faculty and students are often confronted with four interrelated issues: (1) How do we guarantee voluntary participation and informed consent? In other words, how do we make sure that there is no coercion for service-learning, especially among vulnerable segment of the population with diminished autonomy or capacity? (2) Is the principle of shared governance being practiced? Is there a strong buy-in by the local communities? Are the host communities equal partners in the education of student participants? Reflecting over the experience with ISLMP students in Chapter 7, for example, the author emphasized that projects "must be appropriate to the needs of the communities and should be identified together with the locals during the planning stage in forging a partnership for service-learning."[24]

A number of capacity-related questions can be asked about each of the major players or partners in service-learning. First, for community capacity, do our students understand the difference between help on the one hand and social development on the other? Or, are we relatively certain that the local communities we serve will improve their capacity by our genuine, active, and sustained engagement? Secondly, for student capacity, do our students have the maturity, skill, and knowledge, to perform the tasks or duties assigned by the agencies? And, finally, for agency capacity, does the placement agency have the capacity to provide monitoring or supervision for students at the service site? Are the agencies' staff properly trained or have the right credentials? Is it faculty responsibility to scrutinize their qualifications or do we simply rely on administration assurances about these oversight issues? Oversight responsibility is a very touchy issue for the agency and faculty.

The case studies in the volume have addressed those questions in varying degrees. On student capacity, for example, Kwok Hung Lai's point is very well taken when he writes about student placement in Chapter 3, "service-learning placements should be tailored to students' needs and their level of self-efficacy. A community service placement that is perceived as too far beyond the student's capabilities will be threatening, and will decrease rather than increase their sense of self-efficacy."[25]

In addition, the concepts of reciprocity, equity and respect have been cited by the authors as the absolute key for a successful service-learning program. Dennis Lee in Chapter 9, while discussing the Singaporean situation in service-learning, cites reciprocity as the key factor in differentiating service-learning from community service.[26] He advises his readers to avoid "the ever-present pitfall of paternalism disguised under the name of service." "Service-learning," he writes, "avoids the traditionally paternalistic, one-way approach to service in which one person or group has the resources, which they share charitably or voluntarily with the person or group that lacks resources."[27] Likewise, in Chapter 10, Jane Szutu Permaul, in assessing the cross-cultural learning outcomes of the W. T. Chan Fellowships Program, raises similar questions: "Is cross-cultural learning a one-way or two-way learning experience? Do the American hosts learn anything along with the fellows?" It is interesting to note how Assumption University students quickly find out that many communities will only allow a stranger to be involved in the community's life through someone they trust. "In our social exposure to hill-tribe communities," Charn Mayot writes in Chapter 1, "we work together with the Mirror Foundation, a local NGO that engages in community development."[28]

Some writers in the book are strong advocates for the principle of equity, making sure that it is the communities, instead of selected individuals, who benefit from the service. Charn Mayot, for example, advises his readers in Chapter 1, "Any service-learning produces a good outcome for only one or two stakeholder group risks exploitation of the rest, and service-learning programs that intentionally or consciously ignore the benefits to other groups reflect an attempt to harvest other stakeholders' labor."[29] It is also interesting to note that the quote has pointed our attention to exploitation issues for the community as well as students. In fact, specific suggestions have been made by several authors about how to honor and recognize community contributions at the end of our projects. Perhaps, similar questions can also be asked about student exploitation, making sure partner agencies do not use free student labor to perform duties that should have been done by salaried employees with no proper supervision, especially duties outside service-learning agreement. With regard to respect, these writers strongly endorse the idea of diversity/sensitivity training for students by faculty or staff in student affairs, as recommended by John Powers in Chapter 5, where students are expected to be prompt, reliable, respectful, and have the cross-cultural competency in a different society.

In teaching service-learning, we cannot avoid asking whether the project is sustainable given the human, environmental and economic resources available locally. Again, we cite Charn Mayot, as an example, who teaches students the "sufficiency economy" theory of His Majesty King Bhumibol Adulyadej, a long-time intellectual tradition in his homeland. At Baan Amphur Muang in Prachinburi Province, as he writes, Assumption students "learn the principles of a sufficiency economy through exposure to the way community members live, information instruction, and by participating in community activities."[30]

Increasingly, in university settings institutional oversight is being established for the ethical conduct of faculty who are engaged in research, especially with regard to human and animal subjects. That oversight is often provided by institutional review boards (IRBs). In addition, various academic disciplines, such as those represented by the American Anthropological Association, the American Psychological Association, the National Association of Social Workers, and the American Sociological Association, have developed discipline-based codes of ethics. Should service-learning programs and centers establish some mechanism or system, such as ethical oversight committees of their own, for oversight of service-learning projects since no formal research is done by service-learning faculty? What is more, because service-learning faculty members come from all disciplines, should each member refer to his or her own discipline's codes of ethics for guidance in the conduct of service-learning? Contributors to the volume do not give ready answers to the issue, but together they have helped start a worthwhile conversation on the topic.

We want to conclude this introduction with a few words about the structure of the book. The essays have been organized into two parts. The first four chapters, despite their institutional focus, have provided readers with a broad sweep of the history, definitions and methodologies of service-learning in the United States and Asia. In Chapter 1, Charn Mayot gives a brief but accurate overview of the service-learning movement in higher education, which should be quite helpful to those readers who are new to the concept. Chapter 2, by faculty and administrators from ICU, the institution that has taken a leadership role in developing service-learning programs in Asia, furnishes a brief history of service-learning in the region. Kwok Hung Lai, in Chapter 3, offers readers a comparative perspective on the history of service-learning in the North American and Hong Kong contexts. The various examples that he cites, ranging from institutions in the United States to the seven local universities in Hong Kong, show his breadth of knowledge and rich experience in service-learning. In addition, Lai's detailed account of the different components of service-learning, including institutionalization and assessment, could serve as useful guidelines for faculty training. In Chapter 4, J. Chithra and Helen Mary Jacqueline provide a catalogue for the different service-learning models, including discipline-related, course-related and module-related service-learning.

Each of the six chapters in Part II presents a case study, based on a specific location (country or region), program, or model of service-learning. In the first article in this section, John Powers offers a detailed account of a five-year pilot CBI Program funded by the Hong Kong government's University Grants Committee. As the principle investigator (PI), Powers specifically looks at the program's daily activities with regard to the program's key constituencies, namely, faculty, students, NGOs and government agencies. If Powers' essay is institutional in focus, Jens Mueller and Dennis Lee's work in the following chapter has a disciplinary anchor on business and management education on an international scale. Through a large electronic survey, they analyzed the data collected from 477 service-learning participants in Korea, Singapore, China, Australia, New Zealand, Germany, and the United States. In Chapter 7, Enrique Oracion provides one of the most well-documented case studies in the volume, a 2006 study of the ISLMP program hosted by Silliman University in the Philippines. Chapter 8 by Jen-Chi Yen and Bai-Chuan Yang is a field report from Fu Jen Catholic University, one of the leaders in service-learning in Taiwan. As indicated by the title, Chapter 9, by Dennis Lee, focuses on the Singaporean experience in service-learning, which explores varied curricular designs and ways of learning by doing. Using David Kolb's experiential learning theory as its methodology, Jane Szutu Permaul, in the final chapter of the book, reviews the effectiveness of the W.T. Chan Fellowships Program sponsored by the Lingnan Foundation in the United States. After a careful outcome analysis of this 5-1/2-month-long program among seven cohorts of fellows, she enthusiastically endorses the program as a useful model for other cross-cultural service-learning projects.

In closing, our intent in this introduction is to provide some general information about the thematic focus and organization of the book. We also want to acknowledge the Office of Service-Learning (OSL) at Lingnan University for bringing these international service-learning scholars together at the 1st and 2nd international service-learning conferences co-sponsored by Lingnan University and the United Board for Christian Higher Education in Asia. We reserve our final comments for the authors. The contributors selected are a distinguished group of international scholars from Thailand, Japan, Hong Kong, India, Singapore, New Zealand, the Philippines, Taiwan and the United States. In addition, some of our contributors have also served in the roles of community leaders and social workers. Because of its multinational, cross-disciplinary and comparative nature, this book should make a unique contribution to the field of service-learning. On the surface, you may find the collections of essays vary widely in style and substance, ranging from short data report to well-documented critical analysis. But, together, they combine to present a multifaceted field report of service-learning in Asia that allows its service-learning scholars and practitioners to appreciate their past accomplishments and plan for an even broader movement of "Serving to Learn and Learning to Serve" in Asia.

Part I

Variations in Meaning and Forms

1 | Bridging Classrooms to Communities in Service-learning Programs

Charn Mayot

One of the key purposes of education is to prepare citizens to live good lives in their communities. Education in schools, colleges, and universities is generally conducted in classrooms where learners' great minds are enclosed by four walls and confined by the contents of textbooks, instructors' mindsets, and classroom regulations. When education provides an opportunity for learners to link classroom experience to the world in various contexts, their learning can be more meaningful for them and useful for others. Since experience is the basis of learning whereby knowledge is created by a combination process of grasping and transforming experience (Kolb 1984, 41), higher education must teach students how to learn beyond the classroom (Berry 1990). Service-learning, the pedagogy of experiential learning that combines service and learning in a community setting, can be a solution.

This chapter explores the concept of service-learning and its development in the West and in Thailand. The experience of integrating service-learning as a co-curricular activity at Assumption University in Thailand is provided as an example of how service-learning is carried out and how it affects learners, teachers, and educational institutions.

Definition of Service-learning

Service-learning allows students to provide services to others, usually in less advantaged communities, and to participate in community development. Through community service, students provide appropriate services to alleviate societal problems, poverty, and pain. Service-learning empowers individuals and the community and simultaneously "determines the purpose, nature and process of social and educational exchange between learners (students as service providers) and the people they serve" (Stanton 1990, 67). Rhoads comments that service-learning "has a direct connection to academic mission" (1998, 277–297). Service-learning helps students develop through thoughtful, systematic, and loosely structured academic-based services. It is an educational tool used to achieve the desired results of multiple educational goals, such as building academic skills and values (Indiana Department of Service Learning Education 1998). Stephen Brookfield (1983, 16) summarizes the concept of service-learning in two contrasting senses: (1) learning undertaken by students in which they are given an opportunity to have a "direct encounter with the phenomena being studied rather than merely thinking about the encounter, or only considering the possibility of doing something about it" (Borzak 1981, 9, as cited in Brookfield 1983, 16) and (2) "education that occurs as a direct participation in the events of [everyday] life" (Houle 1980, 221, as cited in Brookfield 1983, 16).

Service-learning bridges theory and practice. Social exposure through service-learning gives learners an opportunity to live and participate in community activities and thereby broaden their world views, understand different cultures, and learn about the community's way of life. Martin P. Komolmas, president emeritus of Assumption University, considers experiential learning equally important to learning that takes place inside the classroom. Nevertheless, service-learning is not expected to replace but to enhance and supplement traditional modes of learning.

Development of Service-learning

The history of service-learning can be traced back to the early formation of higher education in the United States. Woodrow Wilson (1902), former president of Princeton University, made a comment that "it is not learning but the spirit of service that will give a college a place in the annals of the nation" (Woodrow 1902, 270). This same idea was echoed at the time of the founding of Harvard College in 1963 when it was noted that higher education should be "preparing citizens for active involvement in community life" (Smith 1994, 55, as cited in Hunch 1998, 5). Although the term "service-learning" was not coined until 1967, when Sigmon and William Ramsey introduced it at the Regional Education Board, the spirit was clearly embodied in higher education's early foundation.

Since the early 1970s, attempts were made to establish a service-learning network and integrate service-learning into the syllabi of colleges and universities. These endeavors met with little success until 1985 when Campus Compact, an organization of college and university presidents, agreed to encourage and support academically based community service at their institutions. During this period, the service-learning movement was strengthened by the Campus Out-Reach Opportunity League (COOL), a group of recent college graduates who were willing to support student-initiated service projects through a program titled COOL's Critical Elements of Thoughtful Community Service. In 1987, the National Society for Experiential Education, with the financial support of the Johnson Foundation, made a serious attempt to articulate and refine a set of best practices. *The Principles of Good Practice in Combining Service and Learning* was completed in 1989 during the Wingspread Conference. This set of service-learning good practices was rearticulated and redefined in the late 1990s at another Wingspread Conference. National support of service-learning was seen during President George H. W. Bush's administration and was concretized in the passage of the National and Community Service Trust Act of 1990. This agenda was recognized nationwide by the presidential campaign conducted by the White House Office of National Services and Points of Light Foundation during President Bill Clinton's administration. To strengthen the movement, Clinton issued a letter on September 8, 1994, to all colleges and university presidents to "inspire an ethic of service across the nation" (Kozenracki 2000). This move inspired the American Association of Higher Education and Campus Compact to convene the Colloquium on National and Community Service in January 1995.

Implementing Service-learning at Institutes of Higher Education

The American Association of Community Colleges (AACC), financially subsidized by the Corporation for National Service, initiated and developed a campus-based service-learning program in 1994. Currently, AACC's clearinghouse is an authoritative resource center for service-learning programs. Service-learning can be integrated into any academic curriculum (AACC 1998). According to a national survey in 1995, 80% of community colleges are either actively pursuing or interested in offering service-learning at their campuses.

Various types of service-learning in higher education institutes include (see also Jacoby 1996, 109–228):

- One-time and short-term service-learning experiences that are integrated as partial fulfillment of a regular course, such as a one-day or half-day volunteer project.
- Co-curricular service-learning that is integrated as part of regular course or in tandem with a regular course.

- Service-learning within the curriculum that is intended to achieve particular educational objectives such as moral development, social responsibility, or leadership.
- Intensive service-learning experiences during which students break away from classrooms or even from home to become immersed in a certain community. The duration varies and may encompass a week, a month, a semester, or a summer vacation.
- Post-college service-learning experiences such as volunteer programs targeted to college graduates.
- Optional extra-curricular activity to which interested students can volunteer their time.

According to a Campus Compact survey among its members in 1994, administrative units that host service-learning in higher education include student affairs and student activities centers, religious programs and campus ministries, career centers and internship offices, academic departments, joint programs between academic and student affairs, or presidents' offices.

Service-learning in Thailand

The history of higher education in Thailand can be traced back to the reign of King Chulalongkorn (King Rama V, 1868–1910) who, in 1902, donated a piece of land in the compound of his palace to establish the Royal Pages School to train and educate the children of royalty and nobility. The first official university of the country, Chulalongkorn University, was officially inaugurated in 1917. During the first 50 years of the twentieth century, the creation of schools and universities focused on specialization within a particular profession or discipline, but also linked higher education to community needs. The traditional missions and functions of Thai universities emphasize teaching and research, provide academic services to communities, and preserve Thai arts and culture. According to the National Education Act of 1999, academic service to communities is one of seven standards that higher education institutes must prove to the external quality assessment committee of the Office for National Education Standards and Quality Assessment.

Although the term "service-learning" was not recognized in Thailand until the early 1990s, social concern has been part of higher education in the country for a very long time. During the 1960s and 1970s, university students' engagement in the community took two forms: community service and social exposure. Interested students volunteered for either social development camps or social exposure organized by student clubs during their summer vacation

(April to May). In the beginning, these experiences were initiated by students and they had to raise funds for their social activities. In the late 1980s, the Office of Higher Education, non-government organizations (NGOs), and the university in which they studied financially supported the students' efforts. Students' social activities during the period were dominated by a development paradigm, and their main activities were to build or renovate a building for a school or a community and organize recreation activities for children. In early 2000, Payap University and Assumption University integrated the concept into their educational systems. The concept of service-learning was sharpened in Thailand at the 22nd International Conference on Service-learning sponsored by the International Partnership for Service-learning and Leadership. The conference was held at Payap University in Chiang Mai, Thailand, January 3–10, 2004. The experience of sharing with participants from other countries helped Thai educators to move forward in this area. Since 2005, businesses such as KPMG, Krung Thai Bank Plc. Co. Ltd., Government Saving Bank, and Siam Commercial Bank Plc. Co. Ltd., have been involved in supporting university students' social projects. Support from the business sector stems from public awareness of corporate social responsibility in Thailand. Businesses do not use the term "service-learning" in their public relations communications; instead, they coin their own terms. Universities and students have been positive about corporate involvement for various reasons, such as financial support, competition, intensive presentation training, public recognition, and increased postgraduate employment. The way the projects have been handled and the objectives of the projects meet service-learning criteria.

Service-learning at Assumption University

Service-learning at Assumption University is organized as part of the Business and Professional Ethics Seminar (BG 1403) conducted by the Office of Student Affairs at St. Martin Center for Professional Ethics and Service-Learning. BG 1403 is a non-credit course that is required for all undergraduate students.[1]

To fulfill the course requirements, students must (a) attend 16 three-hour sessions twice each semester throughout their four years at the university; and (b) fulfill a certain co-curricular activity that includes social exposure and immersion, community service, or service-learning in the first semester of their third year. To complete this requirement, a student must choose a social service project of their interest (organized by the program or initiated by the student, or one the center considers equivalent to the activities it provides) through which they can expose themselves to a community's realities and transfer their knowledge to serve within it. The adoption of service-learning as part of course requirements was initiated in 1998. Between 1998 and 2005, the operation was guided by the concepts of social exposure and immersion, with some attempts to apply the concept of service-learning to the endeavor. During these first seven years, we concentrated on providing an opportunity for students to step outside their surroundings, take the initiative to use their creativity to do something for a community, and thereby see and experience the realities of life. There was limited collaboration with academic faculties in the beginning. After the university announced a clear policy to support and encourage service-learning in 2006, activity coordinators within each faculty were appointed. Formal and informal discussions have been established and substantive cooperation has gradually materialized.

Because moral education is the core function of St. Martin Center for Professional Ethics and Service-learning, community service and service-learning at Assumption University are designed to expose students to community realities; to discover the need to change their value system; to develop a sense of social awareness, responsibility, and commitment; to develop cognitive moral reasoning through analyzing social problems; and to develop a sense of respect for the personhood of others through interaction with people in various social and economic conditions, especially the disadvantaged.

Service-learning process

Three main steps comprise Assumption University's experiential learning and service-learning process: preparation for activities, execution of activities, and reflection.

Preparation for activities: We start our community services and service-learning with two campaigns in the classroom. These campaigns encourage students to discover their interests and find a social activity that will be most meaningful to them. At the end of the second campaign, we organize an exhibition in which they can learn from the experience of former groups and register for the social service of their choice. For about 90% of our students, the activity is a challenge. Their main concerns are what to do, how to do it and whether they can finish or not. During group meetings, our staff members are there to convince them of their potential to accomplish the service work and to assure them we will always be by their side in case of difficulty. We usually spend two to three hours with each group to provide them with information necessary for the type of social service they choose. Understanding the culture of the community is very important. It is a way to respect community members and is the prerequisite for cooperation that paves way for the success of the program.

Execution of activity: At this stage, students work to complete their social service project as planned. This is a moment for the students to step out of their surroundings and take the initiative to do something creative. It also gives them a chance to see and experience life's realities. In practice, change is unavoidable. Unexpected events always arise. For example, students who volunteer to work with disadvantaged children might plan a lot of activities, but they may have to spend half of the time keeping children in order. Likewise, a group of students who volunteer to teach English and discipline to young schoolchildren may prepare a lot of outdoor activities, but on the day it rains, they must adjust outdoor activities to meet the classroom conditions. Or a group of students that volunteer to help the community establish an eco-tourism enterprise might spend a lot of time preparing to teach them about financial management, marketing, and public relations, but on their first visit might discover that time allows them to teach only how to record income and expenses and how to share benefits. Students learn that teaching people in a community is completely different from lecturing in a classroom. They must proceed slowly and community members must practice what they have learned again and again so they will be able to do it themselves.

Reflection: A reflection is a period of time devoted to thought and analysis that allows students to identify and absorb what they have learned. In service-learning, the reflection period is quite important because it is a time for drawing lessons from the experience of performing service work. Our goal is to have an impact on students' value systems. Determining further actions is one good strategy to reinforce their moral senses during a reflection period. For example, one group of students who were exposed to street children in Pattaya were strongly struck by the fact that these children live on 12 baht a day. The students presented an account pointing out that after each meal at home they have fruit to eat, but the children in Pattaya "never taste fruit at all." In comparison, a majority of the students went to see a movie several times a week and spent more than 100 baht for each movie. They wrote that they "had to do something [to get] better meals [for] these children even for a short period." They learned that sacrificing one movie each week could help one child to have meals for seven days. Their campaign on campus in the following month earned as much as 42,000 baht to get better meals for the children. This example illustrates how even a community service project that lasts for only one day can help young students change their attitude towards life and motivate them to be a useful citizen.

Components of Successful Service-learning Programs

Pedagogically, service-learning comprises "head" plus "heart" plus "hands." It is an academic activity done out of goodwill to bring value to a community's people and service providers. Three main stakeholders are involved in the service-learning process: (1) the academy (i.e., college or university, faculty, staff and officials, and board of control), (2) students, and (3) the community (i.e., community leaders, members, non-profit organizations, community-based organizations, and government and public agencies). A program's success is determined by reciprocity, collaboration, partnership, and respect for diversity among these three stakeholder groups.

Reciprocity

Reciprocal benefits to all three parties involved are necessary for a meaningful service-learning program, although benefits gained by stakeholders may vary. Any service-learning that produces a good outcome for only one or two stakeholder groups risks exploitation of the rest, and service-learning programs that intentionally or consciously ignore the benefits to other groups reflect an attempt to harvest other stakeholders' labor. Service-learning programs consume time and energy from all parties involved. Without the faculty's devotion, students cannot proceed in the right direction; without students' commitment, the faculty's devotion is fruitless. Without the community's generosity, faculty and students must remain in their conventional classrooms. As Jacoby (1996, 7) notes, an appropriate atmosphere that fosters mutual benefits among all parties involved is the one in which every individual, organization, and entity involved in service-learning functions as both teacher and learner; all parties are learning and serving each other; and all parties perceive one another as colleagues rather than servants or clients, and do not distinguish between "haves" and "have-nots."

An example of how reciprocity works can be observed by an eco-tourism project made possible through cooperation among the St. Martin Center for Professional Ethics and Service Learning, the School of Management, the Commission for Social Development of Surat Thani Diocese, and the community at Mooban Khanim in Phang Nga Province. Mooban Khanim is in the area hit by the tsunami in 2004. The village was not destroyed because it was protected by a vast mangrove forest around the village. Community members realize that the mangrove forest is both a source of food and a natural wall that protects the community from strong wind and giant waves. They want to protect and preserve it and live with it in a sustainable manner. They shared these ideas with the priest who was in charge of the development project in the area and the priest told them that he would find someone to make their goal possible. When I visited them in March 2009 for the purpose of constructing a learning center for the Morgan children who were affected by the tsunami, Rev. Father Suwat Leong Sa-ard brought me to the village and introduced me to the community's leader to discuss possibilities. After the discussion, they invited me to do a survey. When I returned to the university, I received collaboration from a group of students and the School of Management. Collaboration among the stakeholders led to the decision to take 40 students to the site in May 2006.

In this project, academics have opportunities to meet societal needs and fulfill their institutional mission through work that takes advantage of their scholarly expertise. An eco-tourism enterprise for the community provides professors and students at the School of Management with an authentic scenario to which they can apply their knowledge, skills, innovation, and academic expertise in real-life situations. Results of service-learning experiences stimulate their commitment to their study via a realization of their potentialities developed in classrooms and in communities. In other words, service-learning fosters a lifelong connection among students, communities, and the world through which students learn to address a community's needs, develop and establish potential job links, and use their occupational skills. With regard to values education, which is the main concern of St. Martin Center for Professional Ethics and Service Learning, this service-learning program fosters a sense of social responsibility, respect for the personhood of others, concern for social problems, and commitment to human service (Indiana Department of Service Learning Education 1998). For faculty members, service-learning also enhances the quality of instruction, especially in professional studies, and is intellectually invigorating. Last but not least, service-learning benefits communities through the transfer of intellectual resources via professional services that include technology transfer, technical assistance, policy analysis, program evaluation, organizational development, community development, program development, professional development, expert testimony, and public opinion.

Collaboration

The success of a service-learning program depends on how all three stakeholder groups collaborate. The fact that groups are from different backgrounds and have different interests and expectations does not really matter; what matters most is how they come to the table at which "each voice and concern is heard, acknowledged and addressed" (Mintz and Hesser 1996, 35) at the beginning of the project. In service-learning, difference is not an obstacle as long as it is appropriately coordinated. Moreover, differences can turn into optimal output and outcome because the different skills, knowledge, expertise, assets, and views that each partner brings to a service-learning enterprise can supplement what another party lacks. This is a situation in which the whole is greater than the sum of its parts, because one person's talent and expertise can help another to overcome his/her confinement and limitation. Collaboration cannot be realized without trust and confidence, which is nurtured by an atmosphere of honesty, sincerity, and dialogue. All parties involved must be treated respectfully as colleagues and brother/sisters and invited to voice their needs, expectations, views, and opinions at the beginning of and during the operation.

Partnership

Educational sectors have a great number of limitations, such as financial support, connection with communities, knowledge of communities and their culture, and public relations skills to attract young students to join tough programs. Collaboration with organizations that are keenly interested in these areas helps universities cope with these limitations. The nature of the project determines with which organizations service-learning administrators should seek partnership.

With communities: Service-learning is always operated in a local community, and finding the right community is crucial for the success of the program. Although reciprocity is a must in service, one party often plays a more active role in taking or giving. In most cases, university students take an active role in empowering community members to develop a community enterprise. In some cases, the community takes active roles in sharing their unique experiences to help students learn. In Thailand, we encourage students to appreciate the "sufficiency economy" of His Majesty King Bhumibol Adulyadej. Since this is an intellectual theory with practical applications, exposure to a community that lives by the principles of a sufficiency economy is necessary. At Baan Amphur Muang in Prachinburi Province, our students learn the principles of a sufficiency economy through exposure to the way community members live, informal instruction, and by participating in community activities.

With NGOs: In very remote areas or in a community of indigenous people, service-learning administrators need someone who knows both university context and community culture well enough to help them facilitate service-learning, community service, or social exposure. Many indigenous communities will only allow a stranger to be involved in the community's life through someone they trust. For example, in our social exposure to hill-tribe communities, we work together with the Mirror Foundation, a local NGO that engages in community development.

With government agencies: Direct partnership with government agencies is reserved for projects that concern complicated public entities, such as water ways, national artifacts, and national heritages. We have discovered that to get a project off the ground, partnership with a community, NGO, or interested corporation is always a requirement. However, in an attempt to work with Bangkok Metropolitan Authority to organize an English course for taxi drivers and to develop a canal in the suburb of Bangkok as an eco-tourism site, we have found that communication and coordination with bureaucratic organizations is complicated and time-consuming. The situation could be completely different if service-learning administrators could identify active and committed leaders. Our partnership with 16 schools in Amphur Kaeng Khor, Chaiyapoom Province, has been going on smoothly and efficiently for three consecutive years, thanks to active leadership and a close collaboration with numerous school directors. Our students have organized English and ethics camps for approximately 700 youth, helped develop a flower-growing enterprise within a community, and established a group of farmers who decided to replace chemical fertilizer with bio-fertilizer in three separate communities.

With corporations: Public awareness of corporate social responsibility has raised the level of social involvement within the business sector. Young people in schools and universities are targeted by most businesses through their branding, advertising, and recruitment. A careful study of company profiles enables educators to find a company that is really committed to community engagement. Many businesses have sufficient financial resources and qualified personnel to support service-learning that addresses their policies and helps to link universities to the community. Partnering with corporations also provides a good opportunity for students to see examples of good corporate citizens. In our community project and service-learning in the northern part of Thailand, we have built a partnership with Siam Cement Lampang Co. Ltd. The project has been going very well for three consecutive years.

Respect for diversity and differences

Service-learning is conducted in an outside "classroom" in which students and lecturers must work for success with people from diverse backgrounds. Students and faculty cannot change the conditions, control factors, and/or change the way people interact as they can in their conventional classrooms or scientific laboratories. The diversity issues that students involved in service-learning in Thailand encounter are differences in socioeconomic status, ethics, culture, beliefs, world views, values, age, geographic affinity, sexual orientation, and physical and mental abilities. If this diversity is unavoidable and running away from diversity means the failure of the program, the only solution remaining (if they want to succeed) is to accept, respect, and manage diversity. Diversity is an opportunity, not a threat. It is a situation that enables all participants to learn to cope with differences and come to consensus and/or principled disagreement while defining what is to be accomplished and what is to be learned. Moreover, as Jacoby (1996) suggests, the greater extent to which inherent differences are incorporated, the greater the opportunity students have to grow and succeed. Scholars have suggested the following views toward diversity:

- Diversity is an opportunity to grow as caring, thoughtful citizens in a diverse world (Takagi 1995).
- Human differences are to be viewed in their context, not in isolation or by the standard of one's own perspective, background, and experience (Takagi 1995).
- Synergy can be actualized and developed through a shift in levels of collaboration and reciprocity (Kretzmann and McKnight 1993).

Conclusion

Service-learning is an innovation in education, especially in a teaching university like Assumption University. A shift in various dimensions of education is unavoidable when service-learning is adopted. First, service-learning requires a fundamental change in teachers' roles. In traditional classrooms, teachers assume active roles to provide knowledge and information about the subject matter while students are passive recipients. In service-learning, students take an active part in acquiring information and knowledge by exposing themselves to the real world and by reflecting on their experiences and self. They may experience a change in their value system. Teachers' roles are concentrated on facilitating and stimulating during a preparation period; encouraging, collaborating, and assisting during an activity execution period; and animating and inspiring students during reflective periods.

Secondly, university administrations must be ready to trust their teachers to work off-campus and to evaluate students' performance in a new way. Service-learning requires financial support for items that are not normally included in the daily expenses of a university's budget. Thirdly, students must perform activities that are not simply for the purpose of earning grades. They sometimes must work day and night under pressure and uncertainty in an unfamiliar environment, which is not expected in conventional classrooms. Service-learning programs can be challenging to every party concerned. However, at the end of the program, participants are happy with both what they have learned and what they have contributed to others.

2 | An Appreciation of Cross-cultural Differences through International Service-learning at International Christian University, Japan

Yutaka Sato, Florence McCarthy, Mutsuko Murakami, Takashi Nishio, and Kano Yamamoto

The development of academic service-learning in Asia has been greatly influenced by the activities of International Christian University (ICU) in Japan. While other Asian institutions are also engaged in service-learning programs, ICU has developed a multifaceted approach to this innovative pedagogy. In addition to including service-learning as an integral part of its undergraduate curriculum, ICU has been active in promoting service-learning among Japanese tertiary institutions, in developing networks among Asian institutions for student exchange, and in leading collaborative programs focusing on international multiculturalism. One consequence of these activities is seen, for example, in the changes in ICU students who have participated in service-learning regarding their personal development, career choices, and views of Japan and other Asian cultures.[1] Many of the accomplishments of ICU have been achieved with the help of the United Board for Christian Higher Education in Asia (UBCHEA).

In documenting the development of academic service-learning at ICU, this article considers (a) how the service-learning curriculum and various service-learning programs have been institutionalized; (b) how networking with Asian institutions has been developed; (c) what forms of international service-learning currently operate at ICU; and (d) what lessons can be drawn from the institutionalization of service-learning that may be useful to other institutions.

The Institutionalization of Service-learning at ICU

The development of service-learning at ICU has been successful because it coincides with the mission of the institution and has been supported by strong leaders that welcome its goals of linking academic learning with community-based service. As its name suggests, ICU can be characterized as fostering internationalism (I) and Christian ethics (C) within the context of a liberal arts university education (U). The university began shortly after World War II with the support of Protestant denominations in North America. Currently, the university has approximately 3,000 undergraduate students, which means it is a small institution by Japanese standards. In terms of the actual numbers of students participating in volunteer activities abroad, however, ICU ranks fifth among Japanese universities as reported in the *Asahi Newspaper* (May 14, 2007). The other four universities are all much larger.

The educational mission of ICU is "to educate men and women [as] citizens of modern society serving God and humanity" (Takeda 2003: 115). The university's more recent motto of "Doing Liberal Arts" also suggests a concern with making liberal arts relevant to everyday life and creating a proactive approach to learning through doing (Nishio 2002). Within this context, engagement with the community, both domestically and internationally, has always been part of ICU activities as seen in the ongoing work camps, such as the Thai Work Camp, and field trips organized by the Peace Research Institute.

ICU sent the first students to participate in international internships in 1996. This provided academic credit to students who arranged their own placements with a non-profit organization or non-governmental organization (NGO) overseas and, with the approval of their advisors, spent the summer holidays assisting in the work of the agency. Over time, the internship model was altered to incorporate the principles and practices of service-learning, and specific service-learning classes were introduced into the university's curriculum. In addition, community service was introduced to students interested in participating in local community agencies, local government offices, or regional offices of international organizations.

To date, 445 ICU students have undertaken some kind of service activity. The number of students who participated in either community service or international service-learning is shown by year in Table 2.1.

Table 2.1   Student participation in international (ISL) or community service-learning
             (CSL) by year

	1996	1997	1998	1999	2000	2001	2002	2003	2004	2005	2006	2007	Total
ISL	10	12	12	14	40	68	35	24	24	40	35	33	347
CSL				6	14	20	15	6	11	9	11	6	98
Total	10	12	12	20	54	88	50	30	35	49	46	39	445

Note: The figures for ISL from 1996 to 2004 are the enrollments for international internship, and those
       from 2005 to 2007 are the enrollments for international service-learning.

As can be seen in the table, about 75% of the total number of students did service overseas. Moreover, the table shows the fluctuation in participation over time. These variations are related to developing various programs, establishing the Service Learning Center, and regularizing publicity, application processes, and student enthusiasm for different aspects of service. In 2008, a total of 71 students were involved in service-learning, most of them engaged in some form of international participation.

Figure 2.1 shows enrollments by type of service since 1996. Given the emphasis at ICU on international issues and curricula, the preference for overseas activity is not surprising. Another aspect of the difference, however, may be that Japan is generally considered to be a highly developed country, and it is only recently that the issue-oriented NGO sector has begun to develop. This development is matched by the gradual awareness within the ICU student body of career possibilities in the NGO sector, whether focused locally or international in scope.

With the growing interest in overseas and community engagement, it became clear that students needed to be adequately prepared for these activities. The structure of the academic year at ICU is a trimester system and this makes it difficult for service-learning to be integrated into regular class offerings. The short 12-week terms make it impossible for students to do adequate amounts of service in addition to meeting the requirements of their other classes. Therefore, the development of the service-learning curriculum has been based

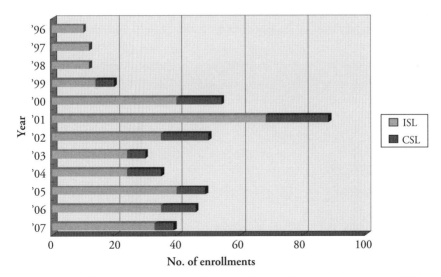

Figure 2.1 Differences in participation by type of service-learning: International (ISL) or community service-learning (CSL) from 1996–2007

on independent, stand-alone classes, with the actual service occurring during the summer holidays.

An initial introductory class was created in 2000 to present students with ideas about alternate forms of service and about the primary objectives of service-learning and its component elements of experience, knowledge, and reflection. Currently seven service-learning classes are offered within the curriculum. These are shown in Table 2.2.

Table 2.2   Service-learning classes currently offered at ICU

Class	Credit	Term
International Service-Learning	3 credits	Every term
Community Service-Learning	3 credits	Every term
Introduction to Service-Learning	3 credits	Spring term
Preparation for Service-Learning Field Study	1 credit	Spring term
Reflection on Service Experiences	1 credit	Fall term
Special Studies in Service-Learning I	2 credits	Winter term
Special Studies in Service-Learning II	2 credits	Winter term

These classes are organized in a sequential manner to insure that students go through the stages of preparation, action at the site, and reflection, as shown in Figure 2.2. Students take the classes in this order: Introduction to Service-Learning, Preparation for Service-Learning Field Study, International Service-Learning/Community Service-Learning, and Reflection on Service Experiences. The introduction and preparation classes can be taken simultaneously because they are both offered in the spring term. Many students take both classes before they do their service activities during the summer and take the Reflection on Service Experiences class during the fall term. For those who would like to know more about the theory and practice of service-learning or about its pursuit in other parts of the world, they can take Special Studies in Service-Learning I and/or II.

Because these are credit-bearing classes, students taking them are expected to meet the same academic standards as for any other class at ICU. Among other criteria, the following are incorporated into the objectives of each service-learning class:

(1) Students must engage in a proper amount of class work.
(2) They are given a reasonable number of assignments.

(3) Their achievements are evaluated properly.

(4) Their service-learning activities are properly linked with knowledge/learning.

Students engaging in service-learning are expected to keep a journal while at their service sites as a means of engaging in ongoing reflection on their experiences. In addition, they are to keep a portfolio of their contributions to their agencies, such as photographs, copies of written memos, brochures, posters, reports, research projects, or other materials that help capture the spirit and form of their service. To earn academic credit for their service, students must prepare a report based on their experiences. This report is submitted to their agencies and is also submitted to their academic advisors for grading. Students also present a 15-minute talk on their service-learning activities to their advisors and the ICU community.

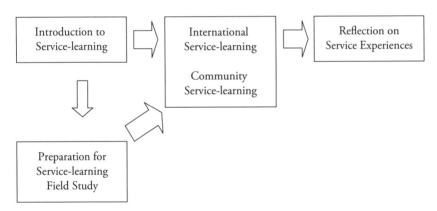

Figure 2.2 Progression of classes at ICU

The Organization of Service

To facilitate students in their applications for service, a Service Learning Center was established in 2002. It is currently staffed with a faculty member who acts as director, a program coordinator who is also an instructor, and two full-time staff members. In addition to assisting the students, the Service Learning Center plays a vital role in organizing the international student exchanges that bring students from Service Learning Asia Network (SLAN) institutions to ICU, coordinating the activities of the students' service-learning network club, arranging meetings of the Service-Learning Committee, maintaining the accounts, and generally managing all the academic and student details in relation to students' participation in service. This includes maintaining a clear set of service objectives and requirements related to parental approval, visas, insurance, and health and security issues. The Service Learning Center has also been responsible for meeting the accounting and expenditure requirements related to a grant awarded to ICU by the Japanese government, which designates the Service Learning Center as a Program for the Promotion of Internationalization of University Education. This grant is designed to foster internationalism among Japanese universities and has provided the funds enabling the development of the International Service-Learning Model Program (ISLMP) hosted by ICU with co-sponsoring universities in the Philippines, India, and Malawi.

The Service Learning Center mediates between students and their host agencies/institutions, and between students and their service-learning faculty advisors. In some cases, the Service Learning Center also subsidizes program fees. The Service Learning Center coordinates the service-learning exchange programs for Asian students who come to ICU to do service, including arranging their service sites, food and accommodation, class visits, and providing an initial orientation and weekly reflections.

To facilitate the coordination of service-learning across the university, a committee of representatives from the faculty and administration has been appointed to serve as a planning body for service-learning activities on campus. The committee meets at least once each term.

To maintain the link between service and academic study, we have created a service-learning advising system. Each student chooses his or her own service-learning advisor based on the type of service, geographical area, and agency type that matches the student's interest. Students are encouraged to choose an advisor who shares similar academic or geographic interests. Often students choose an advisor with whom they have already taken classes. The role of the advisor is to provide academic, experiential, or area-based guidance to students. The advisor usually approves the agency if a student has made an independent arrangement. Frequently, advisors remain in touch with their students while they are in their service-learning sites, and a list-serve facilitates this contact. Advisors are responsible for giving grades to students based on their reports and oral presentations. Moreover, the evaluation given by a student's agency supervisor at the students' places of service is also collected and noted in the student's final assessment. These advisors may or may not be the same as a student's academic advisor.

Networking with Asian Institutions in Service-learning

Networking with Asian institutions was an outcome of a series of conferences, workshops, and meetings hosted by ICU. Two of these were epoch-making: a conference titled Service Learning in Asia: Creating Networks and Curricula in Higher Education held June 30 through July 3, 2002, with funding from the UBCHEA and a workshop titled International Service-Learning Evaluation Workshop held on September 2 and 3, 2005. This networking resulted in the creation of the Service Learning Asia Network (SLAN), with the following institutions as members: American College, India; Amity Foundation, China; Chung Chi College, the Chinese University of Hong Kong; Lady Doak College, India; Petra Christian University, Indonesia; Payap University, Thailand; Seoul Women's University, South Korea; Silliman University, the Philippines; Soochow University, Taiwan; and ICU, Japan.

The purpose of the network is to promote various aspects of service-learning among interested tertiary institutions. Outcomes have included student exchanges among member institutions, the growth of collegiality among faculty members from SLAN institutions, and the development of shared research interests and publications. To foster contact and mutual knowledge about various programs, a web site has been created to facilitate information exchange among SLAN members. Table 2.3 summarizes the history of networking with Asian institutions, not all of which are SLAN members.

Table 2.3 (p. 38) shows that ICU has played an instrumental role in creating networks and starting service-learning research projects and student exchanges among Asian institutions. This emphasis is well within the mission of ICU to promote internationalism, focusing on Asia and Africa in addition to America and Europe. It is increasingly important for ICU students to know and experience the cultures of other Asian countries, to study their histories and economic development, and to learn to work cooperatively with people from these countries.

Another important aspect of service-learning for ICU is a concern for generating a deeper understanding of and reconciliation with its Asian neighbors. A case in point is the conference with people from institutions in Nanjing held in 2007. Nanjing is the site where hundreds of thousands of people were massacred by Japanese soldiers in 1937, and the plans for a reconciliation program in 2009 symbolize ICU's efforts to acknowledge this history. This may be a rather unusual agenda for service-learning, but as nationals of a country that invaded Asian countries and committed atrocities during modern times, creating this understanding is something very important for all Japanese as global citizens.

Table 2.3   Networking with SLAN and Other Asian Institutions

Year	Event
2002	• June 30–July 3: Service Learning in Asia: Creating Networks and Curricula in Higher Education conference at ICU, where it was decided to exchange information and students for service-learning; included 14 tertiary institutions, UBCHEA, IPSL (International Partnership for Service-Learning and Leadership) , 70 participants
2003	• Service-learning coordinators' meeting at ICU, where ICU proposed to exchange students with financial support from UBCHEA • ICU initiated sending students to SLAN institutions
2004	• ICU initiated receiving students from SLAN institutions • SLAN web site created
2005	• ICU awarded a Japanese government grant from the Ministry of Education, Culture, Sports, Science and Technology for further development of international service-learning, covering AY# 2005 through the end of AY 2008 (March 2009) • International Service-Learning Evaluation Workshop at ICU, where ICU proposed the ISLMP, using the government grant • Silliman University, the Philippines, selected as host institution 2006 • Lady Doak College, India, selected for 2007; WSU, Malawi, Africa, chosen for 2008
2006	• July–August: First ISLMP held at Silliman University, Dumaguete, the Philippines; 24 international students attended • September: Second Service-Learning Planning/Evaluation Committee meeting at ICU to evaluate first ISLMP and plan for second ISLMP; began planning joint research
2007	• March, Nanjing-Tokyo Academic Partnership Conference • July–August: Second ISLMP at Lady Doak College; 24 international students and six faculty attended • September: Third Service-Learning Planning/Evaluation Committee meeting at ICU to evaluate ISLMPs and plan joint research within and across SLAN institutions
2008	• May: SLAN Web-Based Research Workshop focused on SLAN research draft papers • June–August: Third ISLMP in Malawi, Africa, co-sponsored by Washington State University, Bunda College, and NGO Total LandCare • September: SLAN Research Workshop at ICU; composition of papers leading to publication
2009	• Reconciliation-focused Service Learning Program for Chinese students and Japanese students

NB: # AY stands for the Japanese academic year, which begins in April and ends in March the following year.

Forms of International Service-learning at ICU

Currently, ICU has three types of international service-learning programs. These involve: (1) sending ICU students to other international institutions or agencies; (2) receiving students from Asian institutions for service-learning activities at ICU; and (3) bringing students from different countries to one location in Asia/Africa for multicultural service-learning experiences. These programs are primarily outcomes of our interaction and agreements with SLAN members, and are managed by the Service Learning Center.

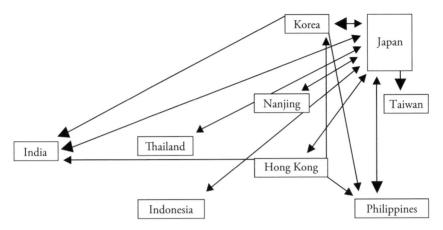

Figure 2.3 Service-learning Network in Asia

As illustrated in Figure 2.3, student exchange among SLAN institutions is increasingly multidirectional and is not limited to an exchange with ICU. For example, Seoul Women's University sends students to Lady Doak College and Petra Christian University and accepts students from Chung Chi College at the Chinese University of Hong Kong. The differently sized arrows in Figure 2.3 indicate that exchanges are increasing among SLAN institutions, and an update of the figure would show even more activity among the institutions.

Economics has influenced exchanges; some countries are more able to send students than are others. The variations in program costs and the cost of living have meant that not all SLAN members are able to be as active in the exchange as they may wish. To assist with this discrepancy, the UBCHEA subsidized the travel expenses of many SLAN students during the first three years of the exchange program. As a general rule, each SLAN institution covers the cost of visiting exchange students, which means that ICU covers the local costs of any SLAN student who comes to ICU. The reverse is true for ICU students going to SLAN institutions. ICU students usually pay their own transportation costs.

ICU Students Doing International Service-learning

Our students go to various places overseas to do service. As mentioned earlier, when international internships first began, students found their own placements and were responsible for arranging the details of an agreement with the agency, their accommodation, and security, health, insurance, and travel arrangements. With increasing levels of insecurity around the world, this free-wheeling type of program was thought to be risky, and so the linkages with established institutions were created as an alternative. While some students continue to establish their own independent arrangements, the recent trend is that most ICU students choose to participate within the context of SLAN.

SLAN institutions provide accommodation and arrange placements for visiting students. Placements are made with local NGO organizations dealing with social issues, providing services, or doing research. The host institution also provides guidance and reflection sessions for visiting students and generally oversees the quality of service. If problems occur, these are readily attended to by local faculty members. In addition, exchange students are often placed with local students if the hosting agency's staff is not proficient in English. We have found that doing service in unfamiliar cultures and working in new environments on problems about which students may know very little provides a tremendous learning opportunity for them; therefore, SLAN institutions' careful selection of local agencies for Japanese students optimizes their challenges in unfamiliar settings that requires students extra effort, insight and patience. We think this maximizes learning related to the placement and its issues while still providing significant opportunities for students to meet and establish friendships with other students, adjust to an unfamiliar culture and setting, and gain confidence in their own abilities to meet these challenges. Examples of the types of service ICU students do abroad are illustrated in Table 2.4.

SLAN Students Coming to ICU for Service-learning Activities

ICU started accepting students from SLAN and other Asian institutions in 2004. These initial exchanges were supported by funding from the UBCHEA and other sources. Students stay at ICU for about a month and have a full calendar of activities. In addition to their service-learning placements, visiting SLAN students are hosted by ICU students and join with them in both social and academic activities.

One effect of the SLAN exchange program is that ICU students have become much more accustomed to the presence of different Asian students on campus. While students from European countries are frequently on campus, it is a relatively new phenomenon to have Asian students represented. In particular, ICU students who have been to the countries and institutions from which SLAN students come are quite anxious to return the generous hospitality and warm treatment they experienced when they were abroad. This means that service-learning students from ICU and SLAN universities and colleges may already know each other, and have ample opportunities to deepen friendships and make new friends. The generous time and energy ICU students give to their SLAN counterparts goes a long way toward making the exchange

Table 2.4   Forms of international service-learning by ICU students

Service Site		Service Activities
American College	India	Service at nearby schools and local NGOs
Amity Foundation	China	Service at a home for people with mental disabilities and the Nanjing Massacre-related museum
Chung Chi College, the Chinese University of Hong Kong	Hong Kong, China	Service at child care centers and teaching English to children with Hong Kong students in Fengkai, China
Lady Doak College	India	Service at kindergartens, elementary schools, orphanages, and issue-oriented NGOs
Nanjing University	China	Teaching English with Nanjing University students at high schools in a rural area
Payap University	Thailand	Service for the elderly, street children, and HIV patients, and mentoring and caring for orphaned children
Petra Christian University	Indonesia	Service in the Community Outreach Program focused on joint projects in rural villages
Seoul Women's University	Korea	Teaching Japanese culture and language in children's programs and at a free school and school for children with mental disabilities
Silliman University	Philippines	Service at NGOs and local agencies doing various activities such as building houses, providing child care, assisting with nursing, and making bricks
Soochow University	Taiwan	Service at youth service centers and youth culture camps with Soochow University students

successful. The number of students coming to ICU from SLAN institutions is shown in Table 2.5 (p. 42).

Although not all of our SLAN partners have sent students to ICU, it is our intention to make sure that students from all SLAN institutions have the opportunity to come to ICU at some point.

Visiting SLAN students are housed on the ICU campus and are close to the Service Learning Center and classroom buildings, library, student union, and other campus facilities. Depending on the term the SLAN students are on campus, they have the option of attending various service-learning classes or sitting in lectures. Regardless of the term, SLAN students have a series of meetings with the Service Learning Center staff that include an orientation program and weekly reflection sessions. The students have a busy and usually happy time attending social events such as a welcoming party, weekend trips, a cultural night, and a farewell party, in addition to other informal gatherings.

The locations to which SLAN students are sent is somewhat limited because most Japanese organizations do not function primarily in English and

Table 2.5   Students accepted from SLAN institutions 2004–2008

Year	Term	Institution	Number
2004	Spring	Payap University (Thailand)	2
	Summer	Lady Doak College (India)	2
2005	Spring	Lady Doak College (India)	2
	Summer	Chung Chi College (Hong Kong)	2
2006	Winter	Seoul Women's University (Korea)	2
	Spring	Lady Doak College (India)	2
2006–07	Winter	Petra Christian University (Indonesia)	2
2007	Spring	Nanjing University (China)	2
	Autumn	Silliman University (Philippines)	2
2008	Spring	Nanjng Normal University (China)	2
		Total	20

it is necessary to have service sites where the staff can speak English and provide the guidance and supervision needed to make the placement successful. Table 2.6 illustrates the kinds of placements SLAN students have experienced.

As part of their program at ICU, SLAN students must prepare a report based on their activities and submit it to the Service Learning Center program coordinator after they complete the program. They are also encouraged to keep a journal of their experiences.

Multicultural International Service-Learning Model Program

Beginning in 2006, ICU began a service-learning summer program based on the concept of *kyosei* or multicultural symbiosis. This theme was included in a proposal to the Japanese Ministry of Education, Culture, Sports, Science and Technology with the purpose of increasing the international orientation of ICU students and faculty. The proposal, which was funded by the ministry, is a three-year grant that promotes multicultural understanding through month-long service-learning programs. Known as the International Service-Learning Model Program (ISLMP), the program is organized with the cooperation of SLAN partner institutions and features students from SLAN institutions who participate together in service-learning activities, including a three-day orientation program, weekly reflection sessions, and placement at service sites arranged by the co-host SLAN institution.

The first ISLMP was co-hosted and organized by Silliman University in Dumaguete, the Philippines, and the second was co-hosted and organized by

Table 2.6 Types of service participated in by SLAN students at ICU

Service Site	Service Activities
Kobokan	Caring for schoolchildren after school hours, inviting community elderly people for various events, participating in child care programs
Asian Rural Institute	Farm work with trainee leaders from Asia and Africa, lessons in sustainable agriculture, participating in cooking
Tokyo International Learning Community	Mentoring young challenged learners in basic literacy skills and social skill development activities, assisting teachers

Lady Doak College in Madurai, India. In both cases, 20 to 24 students from six countries were divided into eight multicultural teams to work and live together at service sites. A key to the success of the program was the collaboration with other SLAN institutions in planning and executing the program. The faculty and staff of Silliman University and Lady Doak College did a masterful job in arranging the schedules, placements, amenities, and programs for the students. Their sensitivity to the cultural differences which their own and other cultures posed to the participating students meant that any problems arising from cultural misunderstanding were handled immediately and with a positive resolution for all parties.

The ISLMP provides multiple forms of new cultural experiences for students, such as getting to know students from other countries; adjusting to a new host culture and institution; adapting to new climatic conditions, language, food and local customs; and, of course, the experience of working as a team member in a local NGO or service agency. To assist with language and cultural differences that existed between the international students and the local environments in which they lived and did their service, the host institutions included local students in the program who could mediate the social and cultural situations of the villages and rural countryside where the students were placed. In the month-long program, students spent about three weeks in local settings doing their service. On weekends, they returned to the main campus for reflection and a recreation or cultural program. Faculty from participating SLAN institutions also attended the program at various times. This gave them a first-hand sense of how the program was going and allowed them to check with their students and develop ties with other faculty. Table 2.7 shows the institutions and the numbers of students and faculty and staff who participated in the ISLMPs.

As part of the assessment of each summer program, a workshop was held at ICU in the months following completion to evaluate how the program had gone; suggestions were made for the next program, and in this way successive

Table 2.7   Participants in ISLMPs

Institution	SU-ICU ISLMP 2006	LDC-ICU ISLMP 2007
ICU (Japan) Sponsor	6 (5)	6 (4)
Seoul Women's University (Korea)	2	4 (1)
Chung Chi College (Hong Kong)	2 (1)	4 (1)
Soochow University (Taiwan)	1 (1)	
Silliman University (Philippines)	Host institution 8 (8)	
Petra Christian College (Indonesia)		
Payap University (Thailand)		2
Lady Doak College (India)	1 (1)	Host institution 6 (6)
American College (India)		2
Amity Foundation (China)		
Nanjing University (China)		
Total	**20 (16)**	**24 (12)**

Note: The numbers in parentheses reflect faculty/staff who participated, and the other numbers reflect the students who participated.

programs benefited from the experience of the others. In addition, a joint research project was designed to ascertain students' reactions and learning from their experiences. Joint questionnaires were prepared and used in assessments. These data will contribute to the final report to the Japanese government and will be the basis for journal articles and other publications.

During the summer of 2008, the ISLMP was held in Malawi, Africa. Washington State University, Bunda College, and the NGO Total LandCare co-sponsored the program. This program followed a format similar to the prior programs, however, because Africa is not as familiar to ICU faculty and students, particular care was taken to create cultural knowledge and sensitivity among ICU students through workshops and lectures before they left for Malawi. Other changes included the participation of a few American students and engaging students in field research related to the needs of Total LandCare to evaluate the results of various projects. The research was related to new cooking stoves introduced in the Total LandCare project area.

Lessons Learned

The lessons learned from our experiences can be divided among those related to the design and institutionalization of service-learning at ICU and those specific to the SLAN network and shared programs. Successful service-learning has occurred at ICU because the objectives of service-learning meld with the mission and aims of the university. In addition, interest in improving the quality of undergraduate education at ICU means that there was and continues to be support for service-learning among faculty and administrators. Much of the responsibility for carrying the administrative and programmatic details of service-learning is borne by the Service Learning Center, which means faculty is not burdened with this aspect of the program. It is important to note that supporting service-learning need not present a great cost to faculty. Also, developing service-learning classes and consistently emphasizing reflection as the keystone linking learning to experience has been important to the program's success. The role of ICU students in promoting the program through word-of-mouth to other students, the presence of other international service-learning students on campus, and the Service-Learning Student Network have all made important contributions to the strength of service-learning.

In regard to networking and the international connections that have come through SLAN, a number of factors made a difference in creating a strong program. One factor is the spirit of cooperation and enthusiasm among SLAN members. SLAN has been a cooperative venture from the very beginning and ICU has been active in promoting this aspect of the network. In addition, the effort to generate joint research projects that focus on the internal assessment of each institution's service-learning efforts in addition to focusing on shared projects means that information generated about the student outcomes for service-learning can be fed back to the institutions. Research also helps reinforce the academic aspects of service-learning. This is an important but often forgotten element in the institutionalization of service-learning programs.

Additionally, a crucial element in the success of the International Service-Learning Model Program has been the strong cooperation among the program co-sponsors with ICU. Careful planning, meticulous program implementation, and the care and concern of participating faculty have been essential. Essential programmatic elements include clear enunciation of the purpose and goals of the program, consistent follow-through for the students in linking their everyday experience to reflective activities, and the thorough supervision of the students' activities in their placements. Key to all of this, of course, is the shared understanding about what service-learning is, and the participating faculty's knowledge and experience with service-learning as it is implemented on their own campuses. The service-learning student exchanges, workshops, conferences, and multicultural programs have all served to bring faculty together from across the participating SLAN institutions and this, too, has been an important outcome of our shared endeavors.

3 | Building Students' Total Learning Experience through Integrating Service-learning into the Teacher Education Curriculum[1]

Kwok Hung Lai

According to the recently endorsed *Development Blueprint* of the Hong Kong Institute of Education,[2] fostering students' professional excellence through building their total learning experience for whole person development is one of the five strategic areas that the Institute will address in the next 10 years. To achieve this goal, students are required to make plans for and take action on various areas to complement their academic studies. One important area is active engagement in serving the community through involvement in service-learning projects, both as participant and organizer of activities for the purpose of preparing for more extensive civic and social engagement (The Hong Kong Institute of Education[hereafter HKIEd] 2007, 34–35). In the Institute's *Strategic Plan 2006–2012*, community service is also identified as one of the sub-themes within "Collaborating with the Community" (HKIEd 2006, 14–17). To recognize students' involvement in serving the community, their service hours are recorded in the Awards and Co-curricular Activities Transcript (ACAT) under the category of Community Service. The purpose of this chapter is to explore various ways of launching service-learning projects, discuss the arguments for integrating service-learning into the academic curriculum as a part of the mandatory requirement for graduation or a credit-bearing educational experience, and to suggest how this can be implemented.

What Is Service-learning?

Service-learning is a form of experiential education in which students engage in activities that address human and community needs, together with structured opportunities intentionally designed to promote student learning and development (Jacoby 1996, 5). It is intended to enrich classroom knowledge by providing activities that stimulate personal transformation, generate greater understanding of the needs of others, and promote social and political engagement (Campbell 2000, Fitzgerald 1997, Hunter and Brisbin 2000, Kezar and Rhoads 2001, Mooney and Edwards 2001, Morgan and Streb 2001). Therefore, it is an integration of service and learning—the integration of community and public service with structured and intentional learning goals (Kendall and Associates 1996, Stanton 1990, Zlotkowski 1996), an effort to combine community service with academic study (Chapin 1998), and a way of teaching and learning that builds academic and transferable skills while contributing to the community. Community service should not be regarded as a supplement to the formal curriculum but as a necessary component of student learning explicitly linked to academic growth. This distinguishes service-learning from volunteer involvement.

In brief, the purpose of service-learning is to provide an opportunity for students to:

1. apply their skills and knowledge learned in class in real-life situations;
2. benefit the community through meeting its needs;
3. become aware of civic responsibility and foster a sense of caring for others;
4. develop a broader appreciation of the abilities, skills, and attitudes required by society to progress and succeed; and
5. reflect on their experiences by thinking, discussing, and/or writing about their service experience. (Lai and Chan 2004)

It has long been known that the effectiveness of learning is conditioned by many factors external to the classroom; systematic studies conducted in many parts of the world (Boyer 1987, Astin 1993, Pomfret and Lai 1999) support this understanding. Through serving the community, the Student Affairs Office (SAO) at the Hong Kong Institute of Education (HKIEd) provides an experiential learning environment for students to actualize what they have learned in class and complement their learning with aspects that are missing in the formal curriculum. This should be seamless with the total learning experience (Lai 2000b). Service experience has been shown to positively affect students' sense of civic responsibility, academic attainment, life skills (Astin and Sax 1996, Sax and Astin 1997), and performance in work after graduation (Pomfret and Lai 2000). Besides serving the needy population, service-learning can further enhance the Institute's collaboration with NGOs, schools, and local, national, and international organizations.

Unstructured real-world experiences have a significant role to play in the design of effective pedagogical strategies and the development of lifelong learners through maximizing students' learning potential by abandoning the often unexamined assumption that significant academic learning takes places only on campus—in classrooms, libraries, and residence halls. Higher-order thinking and problem-solving skills grow out of direct experience, through direct involvement and real-life experiences in workplaces and in the community. This explains why internship programs are becoming more popular as a form of workplace-based learning and some programs are even integrated into the curriculum as a graduation requirement. Like internship programs, service-learning attempts to break down artificial barriers between academic and real-world practice and between curriculum and the co-curriculum. This form of experiential learning engages students in organized service activities designed to meet identified community needs while enhancing students' skills and understanding of course content, rather than limiting focus to extending students' professional skills in practica, work placement, clinicals, and internships (Bringle and Hatcher 1996).

Variations in Organizing Service-learning Projects

Many ways to organize service-learning projects exist, but the three described in this section reflect the author's experiences in promoting service-learning on campus. Students' participation in service-learning is voluntary in the first two and is a requirement for the completion of a course module in the third. The last method appears to be more cost-effective and benefit more students because collaboration with the academics is built in throughout the planning, organizing, and assessment stages.

Long-term service project groups

Long-term service project groups are the most traditional form of serving the community. These groups involve students in training, planning, implemention, and evaluation. Through the development of these service groups, students develop and enrich their leadership and organizational abilities. They develop a strong sense of commitment and identity toward the projects they participate in throughout the academic year. However, not many students are involved and these projects require significant staff input. At the moment, the SAO offers a wide range of options for student participation in community and volunteer services to the mentally and physically challenged, marginal youth, senior citizens, deprived students, ethnic minority children, deprived citizens of the Third World through international humanitarian services, and so forth. These projects are launched collaboratively with NGOs and local schools, and students work with external community organizations to gain recognition from these agencies. During the past five years, the HKIEd was awarded the Caring Organization logo by the Hong Kong Council of Social Services.

Providing a service-learning platform and opportunities

Instead of relying solely on professional staff to organize and oversee service-learning projects, the SAO establishes a platform and provides service-learning opportunities for students through publicizing existing projects developed by external community organizations. It is involved in selecting projects, matching students with appropriate opportunities, and recommending students to service organizations. The SAO also acts as a liaison with external community service organizations to launch tailor-made projects for students. In these and other ways, the SAO serves as an agency to link service-learning opportunities provided in the community with students to match the needs of both parties.

Collaborating with academics

Collaboration between academic departments and student affairs staff is an idea long espoused. It is a general expectation and a reality that higher education must do more with less (Levine 1997). Tighter budgets and downsizing force people from various perspectives to pool efforts and resources, which evokes the image of a seamless, holistic learning experience (Lamadrid 1999, Lai 2000a). More collaborative initiatives are clearly one way to offer expanded services to students at no additional expense, using the combined efforts of teaching staff and student affairs personnel (Lai 2005).

Service-learning initiatives allow department lecturers and student affairs practitioners to collaboratively engage students in an educational process that maximizes student learning and personal development. They encourage natural partnerships between the Institute and the community, and provide students with experiences that address real community needs and include intentional learning goals, conscious reflections, and critical analysis. We can create an increasingly seamless educational process that fosters student learning, involvement, and development. Thus, the learning is more related to the educational objectives of course modules. The author initiated the "Learning through Serving the Community" project by incorporating it into the module on "Creativity, Action, and Service" at the Morrison Hill campus of the Hong Kong Institute of Vocational Education. This was the first time that service-learning was introduced into a module on such a large scale on campus. The role of the SAO was to liaise with local community organizations, to secure placements and service opportunities, and to match students with projects while the departments helped to form students in groups and assess their learning outcomes (Lai and Chan 2004).

International and Local Experiences

Numerous examples of integrating service-learning components into the curriculum can be identified. For instance, the University of Rhode Island, responding to a presidential challenge to develop a new culture for learning, integrated a community service component into a new, one-credit, first-year seminar course. This effort gave rise to a significant challenge for course designers: how to incorporate a one-credit, six-week course servicing approximately 2,000 students in 100 sections and provide each student with a meaningful introduction to college-level community involvement. In a series of focus group debriefings, students reflected that "service requirement had very little meaning," "the service projects had no connection to their course work or career goals," and "projects seemed to be trivial or insignificant." Feedback from course faculty was focused on the fact that "community service had to become a more meaningful part of the curriculum rather than just an 'add-on' and support was needed to put service projects into a learning context." Although there was unfavorable feedback from students and faculty, course organizers revisited their expectations for the service component and came away with a much clearer sense of priorities. Community placements were reorganized around specific themes so that students were provided with materials needed to create a context in which they could understand their service experience. As a result, the course designers were able to make "experiential learning with a focus on service-learning the foundation on which they stood" (Richmond 2002, 69).

Similar to the University of Rhode Island, a service-learning advisory committee was appointed by a chief academic officer of the University College at Indiana University-Purdue University in Indianapolis (IUPUI). It was a collaborative effort to launch service-learning for first-year students of the two universities and to advise faculty and instructional teams on how to integrate service-learning into the first-year curriculum and promote co-curricular service opportunities for new students. Again, it was a top administrator who provided the initial momentum (Hatcher, Bringle and Muthiah 2002). The creation of this "learning community" included an emphasis on group projects, one-time projects, student mentors who were a part of each learning community, and other suggestions regarding project design and implementation.

At Colorado State University, the Service Integration Project (SIP) was initiated by faculty and staff interested in combining community service with facilitated academic learning. Experimental courses were cooperatively designed from the College of Liberal Arts freshman seminars, and SIP staff offered a series of training seminars and coordination of service sites for faculty interested in teaching initial service-learning courses beginning in 1992. Five years later, 41 service-learning courses were offered, involving 1,215 students from 5 different colleges and providing service in more than 50 community agencies. Throughout the development, alliances between academic and student affairs staff was crucial in areas such as providing advice, issuing letters of support, presenting awards, launching publicity, and creating steering committees and programming (Cleary and Benson 1998).

Another example involved integrating service-learning into two upper-division general education death-related courses—"Social Aspects of Dying, Death and Bereavement" and "Topics in Political Theory: Death in America" at Willamette University. The former, a sociology course, covered the classical core of death education, drawing on a well-known body of work on dying, death, and bereavement within its disciplinary boundaries. The latter, a political science course, reflected interdisciplinary developments pertaining to mortality as a criterion in public policy evaluation (Basu and Heuser 2003).

Although these examples are designed and implemented differently, the key to success in each instance is a thorough understanding of students' special needs and the significant difference between traditional community service and academic service-learning.

Various local universities incorporate students' co-curricular involvement as a graduating requirement, although such involvement might not solely be service-learning in nature. Each university has different expectations about students' participation in co-curricular activities in addition to requiring students to complete before graduation. For example, Lingnan University requires students to complete at least 75 integrated learning program units before graduation,[3] Hong Kong Baptist University expects students to fulfill a requirement of participation in a "university life" subject,[4] the Hong Kong Polytechnic University requires students to fulfill the attendance requirement of at least one non-credit-bearing co-curricular activity,[5] and the Hong Kong University of Science and Technology expects all students to participate in at least one organized sport or physical education activity during their years at the university through enrolling in a "healthy lifestyle" course.

Teacher Competencies to Meet with Educational Reform

Hong Kong is now facing unprecedented reform in education. Various changes have been introduced by schools, focusing on the needs of our young people as they journey into a world requiring knowledge and attitudes often very different from those taught to their parents. The rapid changes taking place in contemporary society have meant an end to the sole emphasis on acadmic achievements. Instead, our schools are concerned about fostering whole-person development. Teaching and learning is no longer confined to classrooms, but extends into the wider community.

Generic teacher competencies

The willingness and capacity for lifelong learning we expect from our students should also be reflected in our teachers. As the only University Grants Committee-funded institution dedicated solely to upgrading professional development and teacher education in Hong Kong, the HKIEd needs to reform its curriculum to help students to attain the expectations described in the Generic Teacher Competencies Framework outlined by the Advisory Committee on Teacher Education and Qualifications (ACTEQ). Some underlying principles of the framework include: (1) the recognition that comprehensive development for teachers is as important as it is for students; (2) collaboration and networking are essential in improving teaching effectiveness; and (3) schools are prominent contributors to the wider community. The framework places education-related community service and volunteer work within one of the four core domains of professional competencies—"Professional Relationships and Services." In this domain, teachers are expected to interact with the broader community and participate in education-related community service and volunteer work. In fact, service-learning opportunities and experiences also enable prospective teachers to develop the core values that underpin the Teacher Competencies Framework, especially, (1) love and care for students; (2) respect for diversity; and (3) collaboration, sharing, and team spirit. In other words, institutions focusing on teacher education need to place emphasis on enhancing students' ability to attain these professional competencies through education-related service-learning projects so that prospective teachers will become more aware of the importance of establishing links with the broader community to improve learning outcomes and develop students' positive social values. Students need to be ready to participate in district projects, volunteer work committees, and so forth, when invited (ACTEQ 2003). This service-learning is best implemented if it is already integrated as part of the teaching education curriculum.

New Senior Secondary Curriculum

To produce quality educators with a professional commitment to nurture Hong Kong's young people and to meet challenges and changes brought about by education reform that fosters students' all-round development, it is necessary to provide prospective teachers with the necessary skills and knowledge to encourage students to develop "other learning experiences" as proposed in the new senior secondary curriculum framework (Education and Manpower Bureau 2005).

HKIEd development blueprint

The value of well-organized service-learning to students' whole-person development is undebatable. However, whether this should be incorporated into the curriculum and treated as a mandatory requirement is controversial. Volunteerism and community service are often seen as activities that are peripheral to academic pursuits. Sometimes, service without academic ties is subject to criticism and is questioned as to whether it is a legitimate use of faculty and students' academic time, even though the personal growth and citizenship ethics gained from serving others is generally accepted. Academics prefer to encourage students to engage in volunteer service instead of making it a requirement or integrating it into the curriculum. Service-learning is thus regarded as an extra-curricular or co-curricular activity.

The HKIEd *Development Blueprint* emphasizes the importance of building students' total learning experience for whole-person development. Because this is an integral part of teacher education, the Institute should consider setting clear expectations or requirements on students' engagement and strengthen systems that encourage, support, and give recognition to students' self-initiated and self-monitoring efforts in whole-person development.

As suggested by the Academic Quality Assurance Committee of the HKIEd at its meeting in September 2007, the Institute should explore the notion of "common first-year experience" as used in some universities, and analyze what students would be missing when they enter universities and how universities should make the best use of the additional year in view of the "3+3+4" program development (junior secondary, senior secondary, and university). With the implementation of "other learning experiences" as outlined in the New Senior Secondary (NSS) Curriculum for secondary schools in 2009–10, the Institute should provide broad and balanced co-curricular activities for students to give them the necessary knowledge and skills to meet these challenges.

At the HKIEd Student Affairs Committee meeting in May 2007, student representatives recommended developing measures or mechanisms to promote or require students to attain a certain level of involvement in co-curricular activities. At the Management Retreat that focused on "Turning the Development Blueprint into Action: Creating the Hong Kong University of Education" in September 2007, one of the suggestions collected was that community service and other educational experiences could be built in as program requirements, in the form of credit-bearing or non-credit-bearing modules/courses to foster students' professional excellence.

In addition to supplying foundational and professional knowledge, contemporary higher education advocates educating students to be good citizens by creating and disseminating socially responsive knowledge (Zlotkowski 1998, 361). Simply providing opportunities for volunteer service cannot enable universities to meet students' educational goals for the coming decades. We must clearly regard service-learning as academically anchored instead of extracurricular volunteer work. Service-learning is not simply some form of community service that supports reciprocity between the campus and the community. It is a kind of reflective learning experience with clearly specified educational goals. Therefore, service-learning should be a credit-bearing educational experience with a developed multilayered reflection strategy in which students participate in an organized service activity that meets identified community needs and allows them to reflect on their experience in such a way that they gain further understanding of the course content, a broader appreciation of the discipline, and an enhanced sense of civic responsibility and social justice. Unlike extracurricular volunteer service, service-learning is a course-based service experience that produces the best outcomes when meaningful service activities are related to course material through reflection activities such as directed writings, small group discussions, and class presentations. Unlike practica and internships, the experiential activity in a service-learning course is not necessarily skill-based within the context of professional education (Bringle and Hatcher 1996, 222). We need to integrate service-learning into the teacher education curriculum and treat it as a mandatory requirement for graduation or a credit-bearing educational experience instead of co-curricular or extracurricular voluntary service. In view of these arguments, the General Education Committee of the Institute endorsed the proposal of integrating service-learning into general education modules with the collaboration of student affairs practitioners and academics. Three pilot modules were conducted at the beginning of the second semester in the academic year 2008–09 and positive feedback was received from students.

Components of Service-learning

If service-learning is offered for credit and graded, the first important indicator of student learning is the grades students receive in their service-learning courses. Course organizers need to assess periodically student needs with regard to service-learning, measuring student satisfaction with their community experiences and determining if their learning is in fact related to one or more desired learning outcomes, such as academic achievement, retention, and longer-term goals such as an increased awareness of civic responsibility and an interest in seeking out other community-based experiences. At the same time, we can assess service-learning from a program perspective (Zlotkowski 2005, 368). Collaboration between academics and student affairs professionals in launching service-learning and integrating it with a course module is beneficial to both faculty and students.

The experiences of other countries and local universities have taught us that faculty development and support are critical until instructors have acquired some reliable experience and expertise in integrating service-learning into the academic curriculum. Service-learning assignments provide a foundation for students to learn and construct knowledge as described in Kolb's (1984) learning cycle, which consists of a four-step process: (1) concrete experience involving direct, immediate experience, and a stimulation of the learners' feelings; (2) reflective observation involving intentional observation and reflection on the meaning of the learners' experiences; (3) abstract conceptualization involving thinking and creating generalizations and concepts that organize experience, action, and observations; and (4) active experimentation involving the use of generalizations or theories from the previous step to guide further action. As stipulated in the experiential learning cycle, an effective service-learning assignment should contain four key components: preparation, action, reflection, and evaluation (Rice 1996).

Preparation

In preparing for the incorporation of service-learning into the curriculum, course organizers must visit potential organizations and agencies and select those whose staff are willing to accept and mentor the students during the work placement. It is necessary to engage the potential organizations into contractual discussions to understand the learning opportunities available in placements, prerequisite training required, and the roles and responsibilities of the agencies and the educational institutions. To satisfy both faculty and student demands for academic relevance, service-learning course designers should first consider thematically organized placements and explicit disciplinary connections. In this respect, student affairs professionals can be involved to develop and update a clearing-house of all community resources where students can volunteer.

After making the necessary arrangements with partnership organizations, course designers need to plan for how to integrate service-learning into respective courses. Documentation can include an instructional handout for students interested in establishing a service-learning opportunity, a contract to specify the roles and expectations of all parties involved, a learning journal students can complete to reflect and consolidate their learning experiences, and forms for student evaluation by the supervisor and the site evaluation by the student. These documents can be developed by course lecturers and student affairs professionals together.

Last, but not least, service-learning placements should be tailored to students' needs and their level of self-efficacy. A community service placement that is perceived as too far beyond the student's capabilities will be threatening, and will decrease rather than increase their sense of self-efficacy. Student affairs professionals can pay attention to tailoring the student's service placement if they are involved in negotiating with partnership organizations because they have adequate knowledge of students' abilities and needs and are knowledgeable regarding the needs of specific agencies and the responsibilities involved in volunteer positions (Muller and Stage 1999).

Action

Action refers to both service and learning. Action is the actual work done in serving the community. Students are required to complete at least an expected number of hours of work for the site during the semester, and a certain amount of the work is voluntary in nature. This requires the students' commitment before placement to avoid unnecessary hard feelings.

Knowledge is constructed through engaging in the physical experiences that encourage learners to attempt to understand and interpret phenomena for themselves. Therefore, it is crucial for students to acquire experiences. Course designers, especially if student affairs professionals are involved, should try to help students connect their course-based learning to their community service so they are encouraged to subjectively construct their own knowledge and capitalize on their practical strengths while serving others. The service-learning assignment also provides an environment where students can experiment with behaviors and learn new skills that offer an opportunity for enhancing their beliefs of self-efficacy. These challenges help to shape and actualize their developmental potential. Students may even develop an increased awareness of sociocultural situations. For instance, if students involved in community agencies that foster activism can develop a stronger locus of control, they may develop an increased sense of empowerment in their lives (Muller and Stage 1999, 115–118).

Reflection

Learning from serving others is not automatic. Students serving meals to the homeless, mentoring at-risk youth, and visiting chronically ill patients enjoyed the work and felt satisfied from such altruistic experiences, but did not necessarily engage in critical thinking about the existence of poverty, youth policy, and health-care reform. These experiences may even promote a power imbalance of the privileged "haves" providing for the "have-nots" (Radest 1993, Rhoads 1997, Schine 1995). For learning to take place through service or action, it must begin with preparation and end with reflection, both of which provide the contextual grounding for students. Reflection is the most important means of turning raw experience into usable learning and attaining higher levels of learning and cognitive development.

Students should keep journals about their service, detailing what they observe and experience, and reflecting on how these observations and experiences tie to academic course content. Ongoing class discussions or monitoring visits from student affairs professionals provide students with an opportunity to not only share, but to begin making sense of what they have learned through service. Scheduled periods for class reflection and a final presentation are necessary for students to demonstrate how much they have integrated theoretical concepts with practical service experiences. In this sense, the teacher and student engage in dialogue and are co-investigators in the learning process, and both of them are jointly responsible for learning. Because students are actually experiencing the service provision process, they are allowed to begin the learning process within their own reality, values, and life-situations (Muller and Stage 1999).

Evaluation

Evaluation or assessment comes last and provides the opportunity to ponder how to improve the other three components in future courses (Basu and Heuser 2003). Students' opinions and feedback about their service-learning experiences are usually collected using evaluation forms that allow open-ended remarks. On-site supervisors complete an evaluation form to further reflect how students perform throughout the service placement. Comprehensive ongoing assessment of all stakeholder experiences can help identify problems before they become intractable. Frequently encountered problems may include failure to identify specific service goals, failure to integrate the service experience with other aspects of the class, insufficient student preparation, lack of sufficiently early or substantive faculty contact with the community partner, failure to match the service task with course parameters and student abilities, and lack of adequate on-site supervision (Zlotkowski 2005, 369).

Roles and Responsibilities of Collaborative Partners

The organizational structure of service-learning involves four collaborative partners to facilitate students in meeting their learning needs through contributing to the service practicum. These partners are module lecturer, field instructor, service agency supervisor, and student. The respective roles and responsibilities and their inter-relationships are as follows:

- The module lecturer is responsible for knowledge delivery in class lectures.
- The field instructor is responsible for liaising and engaging with all partners to plan and conduct training workshops to prepare students for involvement in the service practicum, supervising students at practicum sites, and assisting in their knowledge integration process.
- The service agency supervisor is responsible for liaising closely with the field instructor and the module lecturer and provides practicum supervision, orientation, and guidance for students.
- The student is responsible for participating in the service practicum arranged by the agency under the supervision and guidance of the field instructor and the service agency supervisor.

The interrelationships, respective roles, and learning components involved in this service-learning model are summarized in Figure 3.1.

Some recommendations by Zlotkowski (2005, 369) and Basu and Heuser (2003, 915–916) may serve as useful references when the Institute makes plans to integrate service-learning into the teaching education curriculum:

- Carefully and consistently differentiate service-learning from traditional community or volunteer service. Students must have a clear understanding of the learning goals associated with service-learning.
- Design service-learning projects to match and to stretch, but not strain, the students' capabilities. Such projects should build on participants' prior levels of experience. It works best when students themselves select the site and formalize their relationship, rather than being handed a list of pre-arranged possibilities.
- Faculty needs logistical support to do service-learning well. Most quality programs operate in conjunction with a center that facilitates campus-community connections and makes available orientation and

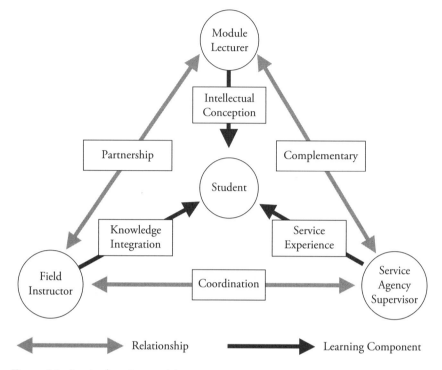

Figure 3.1 Service-learning model

assessment resources. Staff can help students identify suitable service-learning sites and train them for contacting and subsequently serving their chosen agency.

- Provide faculty professional development opportunities, especially with regard to designing student reflection opportunities. Structured group reflection is critical, because it provides students with an opportunity to sharpen their analytic abilities and gives them a forum to voice their questions and concerns, identify common problems, patterns, and themes, and share solutions.
- Service-learning is improved by having a mix of upper-division majors and non-majors who enrich the quality of seminar discussions by trading roles as relative experts in mutually instructive ways.
- Service-learning is more likely to succeed if it has consistent and coordinated organizational support from administrators and student affairs professionals. Without such institutional backing and encouragement, faculty are left with too little time and perhaps insufficient knowledge to create the optimal service-learning experience.

- View evaluation and assessment as powerful diagnostic tools that can ensure that the community's, the students', and the faculty's needs are adequately met.

Conclusion

To meet changes in the New Senior Secondary Curriculum and help prospective teachers acquire the necessary skills and knowledge to facilitate learning experiences as teachers, the HKIEd needs to re-examine the curriculum to incorporate service-learning into the teacher education curriculum. The Institute should make service-learning into a course-based service experience or a graduation requirement rather than a voluntary co-curricular or extra-curricular activity. In fact, service-learning provides a vehicle for the integration of curricular and co-curricular learning as a means of addressing student development. It offers rich and rewarding educational experiences because students learn how to question, probe, and critique what they have learned in the classroom based on what they have encountered in real-life community experiences. Throughout the process, student affairs professionals can play a significant role in working collaboratively with the faculty to integrate service-learning into the academic curriculum. These integrations produce the best learning outcomes in teacher education.

4 | Service-learning Models in the Asia-Pacific Region and Lady Doak College

J. Chithra and Helen Mary Jacqueline

Service-learning is a method by which students improve academic learning and develop personal skills through participating in structured service projects and sharing guided reflections on their experiences. It is burgeoning all over the world as institutions of higher education realize that to fulfill their respective missions they must find ways of connecting students' academic training to the community and its needs. Furthermore, educators now recognize that direct service experience enables deeper, more precise, and longer lasting learning compared to abstract learning alone. Therefore, these institutions are showing keen interest in integrating academic learning with community service by finding ways for students to directly apply concepts learned in the classroom. Service-learning integrates content with context to provide meaningful learning.

Service-learning is not intended to be used in every course, but it is possible to incorporate it into any discipline. It is not possible to design a single model that effectively integrates service-learning into academic study for all disciplines or institutions. Service-learning must be contextualized and relevant to meet unique and evolving needs, and the broader objectives of service-learning provide room for various models to emerge. As institutions find creative ways of incorporating service-learning into their curriculums, we see many innovative approaches in adapting the new paradigm. By creating and evolving methods of adopting service-learning, faculty members have developed different models that allow their disciplines to serve society. Thus, service-learning takes different forms in different contexts.

This chapter reviews a wide range of models practiced in Asia and other countries to inspire institutions to integrate service-learning into their curriculums. The service-learning models discussed here are identified through a review of publications and web sites and special attention is given to service-learning models practiced at Lady Doak College (LDC).

Service-learning Models

The broader objectives of service-learning provide room for various models to emerge. As service-learning promotes creative ways to incorporating it into the curriculum, there are different innovative approaches which are classified as service-learning courses, service-learning projects and international service-learning programs. The service-learning courses are discipline-related, course-related and module-related. The service-learning projects may be problem-based involving an interdisciplinary approach. In the international service-learning programs, students from institutions in other Asian countries serve in a different national culture, which has different values, assumptions and norms.

Discipline-related service-learning

Field study has long been incorporated into coursework in natural sciences, social sciences, and linguistics. Recently, a shift in mindset with regard to field study has occurred and service-learning is being introduced. With service-learning, the target group is necessarily less privileged instead of well-established sophisticated institutions. Students, faculty, community and the service agencies jointly organize service-learning activities.

Service-learning differs from traditional field study in that it is a separate program of the department or discipline and the comprehensive knowledge gained through coursework is applied to community service. Traditional learning by observation can be seen as exploitative because the student is the only one who gains. In service-learning, the beneficiaries are both students and the community. Students, faculty and service agencies jointly organize service-learning opportunities and students become working members of the community.

Course-related service-learning

In this model, service-learning is tied to one particular course within the degree program. It is a created study that is especially designed for the service experience and must be completed to earn credit for the course. It may involve multidisciplinary or interdisciplinary content. Interested students register for the service-learning component of the course as an option and earn additional academic credit after completing the service-learning assignments.

Cohesive curriculum

In a cohesive curriculum, two or more disciplines are brought together around a service opportunity. The service may be a group project and it may be problem-based. For example, a curriculum that addresses the pollution of drinking water in a community might bring together points of view from biology, economics, engineering, chemistry, and sociology to examine the cause of the problem and arrive at a solution. Cohesive curriculums demonstrate collaborative teaching and learning and thus require a coordinated approach to problem solving.

Module-related service-learning

Under this model, service-learning is incorporated into a course and the knowledge gained through one module (i.e., one unit) is applied to service. The model is most appropriate for multidisciplinary courses. It gives faculty and students the flexibility of fulfilling several core disciplinary competencies in a course and allowing students to design their service-learning projects to meet the learning outcome requirement of one specific unit or module.

International/intercultural service-learning

Although most service-learning programs start with local communities, the call for global literacy and world citizenship has motivated service-learning teachers and practitioners to expand their programs overseas. When the students serve in a national culture that is different from their home culture, they are exposed to new values, assumptions, norms and perspectives. Added benefits are numerous. For example, students are able to learn concepts such as power distance, uncertainty avoidance, and high- and low-context communication styles.

Lady Doak College Service-Learning Models

Lady Doak College has been committed to learning for 60 years. The mission of the college is to impart holistic education based on the values of love, justice, equality, and peace in young women from all strata of society and to enable them to develop as intellectually mature, morally upright, socially responsible, and spiritually inspired national leaders. The learning process and experiences are intended to liberate, transform, and empower the learner and the learned. Since its inception, Lady Doak College has placed a strong emphasis on values education and service programs. Programs that, for instance, take science to villages and promote literacy were actually service-learning programs before the concept was formally introduced. The programs, offered in stages, serve as a foundation for the students. Values-based courses help them to understand themselves and their environment. The service programs cultivate an aptitude for service and help students become responsible citizens and empowered leaders.

Institutionalization is a process by which an activity or program becomes a permanent part of an organization. To attain the objectives of the institution, Lady Doak College institutionalized service-learning, beginning in the academic year 2004–05. At this institution, students apply and validate concepts and theories learned in the classroom to real-life situations, serving the community as an integral part of their course.

Lady Doak College formed a core service-learning team consisting of faculty members from all the departments. The team held a two-day National Consultation on Institutionalizing Service-Learning and invited interested faculty from other colleges. The Lady Doak College core team members were oriented in periodic meetings. At these meetings, team members specifically addressed the faculty's concerns regarding integrating service-learning into the curriculum, and faculty were motivated and challenged for the cause. When the concept was accepted, the departments presented their own proposals.

All departments at Lady Doak College have now designed a course or program that links academic learning to community service. These opportunities are introduced in the curriculum for all undergraduate students, and students who enroll in a service-learning program are awarded additional credits. Service-learning has been incorporated into the curriculum in the following models, recognizing the need to enable academic freedom and innovative learning.

Discipline-related service-learning

Some departments realized that the comprehensive knowledge gained by the students in their discipline through various courses offered by their departments could be applied to community service and hence they framed separate programs. For example, the Department of History created a program called Citizenship Training for Rural Women and the Department of Physics created a program called Help Desk to repair simple experimental devices in the school's science labs.

Course-related service-learning

Some departments identified courses offered in their regular curriculum that could be directly linked with community service. For example, the Department of Mathematics created a Math for Competitive Exams program and the Department of Chemistry created a program called Diagnostic Chemistry.

Module-related service-learning

In some cases, one module (unit) of a course is devoted to service-learning. For example, a women studies course on campus has successfully incorporated a service-learning module on women and health, where students are able to work with local clinics for women and learn first-hand the health and treatment disparities among women in our society.

Applied projects

Applied projects require the comprehensive knowledge gained by students in their own discipline to be applied for service-learning, thereby enhancing their academic learning. Applied projects are often offered in students' final year in school. For example, the Department of Chemistry has incorporated UG (undergraduate) Applied Projects into its regular curriculum. Some of those applied project titles include: "Estimation of calcium and phosphate in water samples taken from ponds," "Estimation of micro and macro nutrients in soils of Natham area," and "Complexometric determination of hardness of water samples." The specific learning outcomes of those applied projects are in the process of being assessed by department faculty and students.

Cohesive curriculum

Lady Doak College implemented the core curriculum model to create two service-learning programs: LAMP (Learning and Application Made Possible) and LAB Serve (a "lab to land" project).

LAMP is a learning center for children from less privileged schools in and around Madurai, India. Its evolution can be traced to the college's early experiences as part of National Service Scheme activities. National Service Scheme students wanted to provide a meaningful learning experience for young children and during regular tutoring visits to the children they noted that several schools had inadequate lab facilities. Under extension activities of the college, a science exhibition was organized for the children. Simple experimental setups, models, charts, and displays prepared by student volunteers provided a meaningful learning experience for the children and enhanced their understanding of scientific inquiry. To provide an ongoing learning experience for highly motivated and enthusiastic children in a centralized place throughout the year, the learning center (LAMP) was established in March 2005.

Students serve as volunteers in LAMP as part of their activity under extension programs. They prepare models, displays, and simple experiments, and contact concerned authorities to arrange visits.

When children visit LAMP, they are taken on a tour of the eco-friendly campus. They visit a butterfly garden, percolation pond, and solar gadgets installed on campus to motivate their aspirations for higher education. In addition, they visit several displays, including:

- A "science corner" that consists of simple experimental setups, charts, specimens, models and small learning kits.
- A "humanities corner" that includes charts depicting the mineral wealth of India, Indian railways, Indian population statistics, a collection of Indian pottery and coins, and so forth.
- A language lab equipped with microphones and computers that enable the children to enhance their communication skills.
- A mini-theatre that includes a DVD player that can be used to challenge the children with multimedia presentations on relevant topics and a CD with educational interactive games to enhance their interests and aptitude.
- An herbal garden that includes a display of saplings and herbal plants with their medicinal application identified.

Lab Serve is a "lab to land" project where the chemistry students learn to use analytical skills to test various consumables used in daily life, botany students prepare nutritive food and test food spoilage, zoology students apply their diagnostic skills to test body fluids, and physics students apply their knowledge of electronics to rectify simple faults in electronic appliances.

International/intercultural service-learning

Lady Doak College students participate in an international service-learning program outside India, and students from other countries participate in a similar program at Lady Doak College. These programs provide cross-cultural service-learning experiences for participating students. The objectives of the program are: to gain a deeper understanding of national/cultural differences; to develop cultural sensitivity by fostering an appreciation for cultural diversity; to increase students' ability to adapt to a situation that is different from their home environment; to enhance teamwork and improve interpersonal relationships across cultural boundaries; to appreciate nature and the cultural heritage of the host country; and to develop reflective and analytical skills.

The host institutions design the program. Students are placed in service agencies to render service. The program at Lady Doak College provides an opportunity to audit an elective course, participate in values-based courses, and learn Indian art. Interactive sessions with students are arranged in the evenings to give them opportunities to appreciate and enhance their cultural and academic backgrounds. Family visits are arranged to enable students to see the social/cultural differences in the country. Celebratory evenings with an international theme give students an opportunity to make presentations on their cross-cultural learning experiences. Students participate in activities held on the host campuses and weekend trips are arranged for the purpose of sightseeing. Service-learning coordinators at the host institutions evaluate the students' performances.

Impacts of Service-learning Programs

When students are exposed to the realities of life, their perceptions change. They are better prepared for community living. They are more likely to develop as responsible adults and effective, influential leaders. Some students who participate in service-learning programs choose social service as a career. In addition, service-learning helps to remove the barrier between students and faculty.

Service-learning builds rapport among local neighborhoods, universities, and students. The community's needs are addressed (partially or completely), and the quality of service to community members is improved. Children in villages are inspired to reach for higher education. The literacy level of the community increases.

Conclusion

Education of the head, heart, and hand is achieved through adopting the service-learning pedagogy. Deriving new knowledge from the experience gained enhances students' learning and improves the quality of service provided by institutions of higher education. A comprehensive orientation and training in necessary skills help students to carry out a service-learning program successfully. Ample choices of service experiences enable students to participate in a program suited to their personal goals, interests, and career options related to their academic study.

Administrators must provide the necessary internal structure to strengthen service-learning programs and provide adequate support for faculty and students. Program coordination is most effective when carried out by a separate center to design the curriculum, plan activities, identify service agencies and resource persons, evaluate students, maintain official correspondence, and provide other administrative services to simplify the functions required by faculty. Faculty can be appointed to attend trainings, seminars, and/or conferences regionally, nationally, and internationally to help broaden their views and involvement.

The various service-learning models cataloged here is not exhaustive for the Asia-Pacific region. Although each of these models has individualized goals, they are all carefully designed to give due importance to the key elements of service-learning: service, learning, and reflection. Attempts to link extension programs with curriculum and institutionalizing service programs are expected to bear fruit in the coming years. It is worth restating that higher education should not be confined within the four walls of the classroom; it should be related to reality and therefore linked to society and its contextual problems, resulting in relevant learning experiences for students.

Part II

Case Studies

5 | The Community-based Instruction Program at Hong Kong Baptist University

John H. Powers

Between September 2002 and July 2007, Hong Kong Baptist University (HKBU) developed a successful service-learning program thanks to a grant given by the Hong Kong government's University Grants Committee to support the implementation of new teaching initiatives. The grant was originally intended to cover the period between 2002 and 2005; however, due to some cost savings and supplementary university support, the program was maintained for an additional two years. To illustrate the distinctive nature of the program as it unfolded and the lessons learned during its five-year life span, this chapter describes the approach to service-learning that was developed in the HKBU project.

Project Origins and Conceptual Foundation

Responding to a broad call for teaching development proposals from the University Grants Committee, a small team of academics at HKBU charged with overseeing different aspects of the university's teaching mission met in spring 2002 to brainstorm. We quickly decided to propose a program in service-learning and I was elected to develop the document. After some preliminary research, I wrote a proposal entitled "Enhancing Whole Person Education through Community-based Instruction," which gradually became known throughout the university simply as the CBI program. The proposal team envisioned the program as contributing to the university's longstanding commitment to whole person education; moreover, we were especially concerned about emphasizing the university's historical commitment to a service-oriented ethos as part of its educational mission.

The CBI program team defined community-based instruction as any instructional practices that are situated in the real-life experiences of the Hong Kong community and which can also contribute to the enhancement of that community as an outcome of using those instructional practices. Accordingly, we divided community-based instruction into two components: service-learning and problem-based learning. Each type of learning emphasizes students' engagement with the community, but in different ways.

For the purpose of the project, service-learning was defined as instructional practices designed to engage students in the life of their communities by combining service to the community with subject content. The principle behind service-learning is that students' knowledge is enhanced by putting it into practice within the community to help accomplish socially meaningful results. In contrast, problem-based learning was defined as a teaching method that builds the instructional process around one or more complex problems that the course content may be used to solve. The goal of problem-based learning is to encourage students to discover how real-life situations in their community may be analyzed into their component elements and to explore how a particular set of concepts and theories (the course content) may be used to approach problems. Combining service-learning with problem-based learning to form community-based instruction, the goal of the project was to enhance HKBU's whole person education by engaging students in understanding how their respective areas of expertise may be applied to developing solutions to a community's problems and how those solutions might be implemented through actual practice on their part. As the project unfolded, the service-learning component became the primary element, growing consistently larger and becoming progressively more extensive because of increasing faculty interest generated through word-of-mouth reports from successful classes. Accordingly, this chapter will focus exclusively on the service-learning dimension of the CBI program.

Essentials of the Service-learning Program

The service-learning program implemented at HKBU had three primary constituencies to attend to on an almost daily basis: (a) the faculty, who had to be convinced that changing one or more aspects of their teaching methods would be manageable without too great a burden on their time; (b) the students, who had to be persuaded that the extra work involved was meaningful and worthwhile; and (c) the NGOs receiving the service, who had to be convinced that the time spent working with students would be rewarded with results that they could not otherwise have achieved in a cost-effective manner. As discussed in this section, considerable effort was required to persuade each of these constituencies, especially early on, and the implementation team needed different skills for working with each group.

Staffing and organizational structure of the CBI program team

Among the most distinctive aspects of the CBI program was the fact that the grant allowed us to hire two full-time staff to conduct operations on a daily basis, one as a project coordinator and the other as a project assistant. The project coordinator held a master of philosophy degree in a communication-related discipline and remained with the project for its duration; each of the two project assistants had strong undergraduate degrees in traditional academic subjects. We know that full-time staff is unavailable for many programs and the work is done by faculty volunteers committed to the values of service-learning, but otherwise only minimally supported. However, as the description of our daily operations will suggest, operating our program without full-time staff would have been impossible.

The HKBU community-based approach to service-learning

The approach to service-learning taken during the CBI program was to have one or more service-oriented elements included as assignments within a regular class. That is, rather than having a separate service-learning class or offering a summer program during which students could perform community or international service outside of their regular curriculum, our approach was to identify regularly scheduled academic classes with course content that could be used to help some non-commercial group or agency within the community. We would then contact the departments and faculty involved to schedule a meeting, explain what we were trying to accomplish in the CBI program, describe the nature of the support services our staff could provide, and then work collaboratively with the faculty to design a service-learning project that would fit the course content and instructor's goals.

Our procedures from the beginning were designed to try to make the implementation of the service-learning component of any class that adopted it as minimally demanding on the instructors as possible. As one might guess, some instructors became quite enthusiastic in engaging the service-learning values, and others were content to let the team design and conduct a single service-learning component while not otherwise becoming very involved. However, we decided early on to accept whatever level of cooperation we could secure from faculty, in hopes that early successes would get around the campus and our reputation could be built in a positive direction over time. As it turned out, this was a very successful strategy.

During the first full semester of the CBI program's operation (spring 2003), Communication Studies Department faculty agreed to serve as guinea pigs, because many of our classes involve applied communication knowledge and skills that might have fairly obvious service applications. For example, students in our digital graphics curriculum could design posters for an NGO, public relations students could help them plan or execute a public relations campaign, and students in organizational communication might help an agency evaluate its internal communication to make it more effective. Many early projects involved evaluating and improving nongovernment organization's (NGO's) websites to make them more user-friendly, visually attractive, interactive, and so forth.

As the service-learning program began to reach beyond the Communication Studies Department in subsequent semesters, instructors in the social sciences were persuaded, for example, that research methods classes could be taught by having students design and implement surveys; the Computing Science Department could have their students write simple but useful programs for the agencies; and philosophy instructors could imagine projects in applied business ethics. Ultimately, nearly half of the university's departments engaged in service-learning projects; examples include Accountancy and Law, Cinema and Television, Education Studies, English Language and Literature, Finance and Decision Sciences, History, Marketing, Religion and Philosophy, and Chinese Medicine. Thus, as we expanded our experience in working with departments, we were increasingly able to imagine service-learning projects for disciplines that would never have occurred to us in the earliest days.

Daily Operation for CBI Program Staff in Project Development

Because some readers will be contemplating the prospect of creating or refining a service-learning program at their school, the types of duties performed by our staff are relevant to understanding the magnitude of the workload and appreciating the accomplishments of our team. The activities described below were efficiently maintained, which allowed the program to continue to grow to its relatively full capacity with available staffing.

Activities related to working with course instructors

When the CBI program staff first began working with instructors, the most difficult part of the process was persuading faculty that the service-learning component we were proposing would be manageable and worthwhile. After all, it takes effort to design new assignments, implement them, and assess their results. This problem was not made any easier at first because, as the principal CBI program supervisor, I was the only one of the three staff members who had actually taught a class and understood experientially the problems instructors faced. We were fortunate, however, that our project coordinator had an advanced degree so that we could arrange for her to teach a class for the Communication Studies Department when an unanticipated opportunity arose. After teaching her own class — and experiencing the type and amount of preparation involved — she was able to speak with considerably more confidence to faculty members about developing a service-learning component for their classes and to address their course-planning issues. Over time, she developed a high level of skill in helping faculty imagine the service potential in the classes they were teaching. In many ways, the opportunity for our project coordinator to teach a class while developing the program was probably one of the most fortuitous aspects of our early development.

As mentioned above, one of our greatest perceived challenges was convincing faculty who had never considered adding a service-learning component to their classes that the time involved would not be too onerous or demanding. For this reason, we rather aggressively identified the kinds of things that a faculty member might require assistance to accomplish, and then we developed strategies that would allow many of those tasks to be performed by our staff rather than by the faculty member involved. Although delegating a lot of responsibility to the CBI program team may seem to be coddling the faculty members, we felt we would get very little cooperation if we did not help facilitate the work of designing student assignments, developing appropriate assessment procedures, identifying relevant cooperating NGOs, and so forth. Some of the many things the staff did in relation to the faculty constituency to facilitate their willingness to try integrating service-learning into their courses included:

- Meet with instructors to introduce the CBI program.
- Discuss possible project details (e.g., discuss issues related to the course, including deciding what types of service activities might be applied to the course; agree on unit grading procedures; establish deadlines and timelines).
- Prepare a syllabus for the community-based education portion of the course (e.g., review service-learning literature for the instructor, clip relevant news articles for the class, collect other types of information as necessary for implementing the service-learning assignments).
- Make follow-up contact by e-mail or phone calls with each instructor to match projects with classes (minimum of 10 to 20 such contacts per class).
- Modify the community-based education syllabus according to instructors' feedback.

- Provide orientation sessions for the students to explain the service-learning assignment so that no class time is diverted for this purpose.
- Prepare grading forms for instructors related to the community-based education unit of the course.
- Prepare forms for instructors to evaluate program results.
- Collect students' products for the instructor.
- Arrange certificate or award ceremonies (e.g., facilitate instructor comments and feedback after a group of students completes the program and after all presentations; arrange group pictures; thank guests with token gifts).

As the list indicates, we proactively made initial contacts with the instructors rather than simply advertising our program and waiting for them to contact us. Moreover, we made a point of investigating the course content of the instructors and departments we were contacting so that we went into meetings prepared to offer concrete suggestions. This preparation included using the Internet to explore what others were doing in specific disciplines. That background was especially helpful in disciplines that did not appear to have obvious service-learning potential. We discovered that others had preceded us and, even more importantly, that we were not alone in proposing certain kinds of service-learning tasks. Having made our initial pitch and receiving nibbles, we did quite a bit of follow-up with faculty to gather more information. Ultimately, based on back-and-forth interaction between the CBI program staff and the potential faculty member, the team was able to propose possible assignments.

Once these assignments were refined and agreed upon, the team helped design appropriate evaluation instruments. These, of course, always involved the instructor's assessment of the value of the work produced based on normal academic criteria; in that regard, we need not have helped the faculty member, but from our point of view, evaluation also involved assessing the work produced based on service-learning criteria. A general consensus in the service-learning community is that the students should learn something distinctive from their service and not just serve. Service-learning is not mere voluntarism. Accordingly, a number of different ways of assessing what they learned from their service (e.g., reflective journals, oral reports, interviews) were designed and used. Moreover, because service-learning projects are always a partnership among teacher, student, and the recipient agency, the team designed certificates of completion that were signed by the instructor, a representative of the agency, and a representative of the CBI program team to recognize the special nature of the students' work. Finally, the team performed the follow-up tasks of thanking the agencies on behalf of the instructor to try to produce a satisfying feeling of completion for everyone involved.

Activities related to working with students

One might imagine that students would be the easiest constituency to engage in the service-learning process; after all, teachers routinely design classes, including teaching/learning activities, and students are expected to complete the activities to pass the class. Moreover, students frequently complain about the relevance of their academic work. What could be more relevant than a service application within the context of their courses? Alas, students were frequently resistant. Performing service is an active process, whereas sitting in a class taking notes is relatively passive; service entails going out to the agencies being served, meeting their staff, learning how they perceive their agency's needs, making a plan for them, executing the service, and so forth. Moreover, there is risk of failure in a quite publicly visible way since, in some classes at least, more than one group from the course could be competing to offer the best service to the same agency.

To encourage students to participate enthusiastically, the CBI program staff met with every student group involved in a project to provide an orientation. They also served as a liaison between the student groups and the agency personnel as needed. Some of the most prominent activities performed on behalf of the student constituencies to make their lives easier were as follows:

- Preparing the special community-based education syllabus for students of each class.
- Providing out-of-class briefings to introduce the CBI program and explain the nature of the service program.
- Obtaining necessary personal information from students, especially contact information.
- Arranging students' site visits (e.g., coordinating with NGO representatives, arranging project times and venue with NGOs, arranging transportation to the sites, accompanying students to the venue, reminding students about deadlines for proposals and final projects, following up on students' work progress and modifying products when necessary).
- Arranging final presentations, usually outside of the class's regular class time.
- Arranging award ceremony procedures (e.g., preparing name cards, boards, pens, evaluation forms, and arranging for such things as water,

glasses, video camera, video tape, still camera, battery, room, equipment, computers, and parking spaces for NGO guests).
* Arranging video recording and photo taking.
* Attending student presentations with the class.
* Serving as master of ceremonies at such public presentation.
* Preparing award certificates and certificates of participation.
* Conducting student presentations, including introducing students in both Chinese and English and describing the work they have completed.
* Collecting students' products (e.g., arranging for gathering instructor comments and feedback sheets after a group of students present their results and after all presentations are collectively finished).
* Sending evaluation forms to students.
* Arranging press interviews and writing press releases about the more distinctive projects and collaborations.

As the list suggests, the CBI program team provided many services to the students to facilitate their success and reward their efforts. Importantly, this included publicizing their successes both throughout the university and in the wider community.

Much of the work on behalf of the student constituency was in serving as the liaison between the student and the service recipients. Such liaison work, however, went far beyond simply facilitating contacts. In many classes, formal presentations of the work performed were required. This meant arranging a meeting time for everyone involved to be together in one place for presentations, evaluations, awards, and recognitions. It meant arranging transportation, including taxis and buses if the agencies were in distant or difficult locations. In addition, it meant publicizing the efforts of the students in local news outlets when the service performed was of sufficient news value to warrant the attention.

Activities related to working with NGOs and government agencies

To my surprise, once we had explained what we were trying to accomplish and had assembled something of a track record to display, the agencies proved to be the easiest group to work with—in spite of the grooming time involved in setting up the original relationships with them. The key problem at the beginning was, of course, convincing them that they would actually receive a usable service from student learners. Of course, they did not always receive an effective service; however, most of the agencies were quite tolerant of the students' learning curve, and word-of-mouth quickly spread tales of student contributions. Indeed, many agencies participated for several semesters in spite of the time commitments involved in doing so.

A second challenge in working with the NGOs was that all student projects needed to be evaluated by the agency representatives (not always as part of the student grade), and this took time; however, in most cases, the time commitment seemed to be quite joyously given. Personnel from the agencies would come to witness competing presentations when appropriate, evaluate them orally, and explain why they thought a particular proposal or implementation was better for the agency. Ultimately, the CBI program team worked with more than 100 different agencies and conducted several hundred service projects during the five-year period. By the end of the project period, we could not serve all of the agencies that might have liked to have participated without increasing the number of staff.

Some of the activities performed by staff to facilitate the service-learning projects with the agencies included:

- sending mass emails to invite NGOs to join our project;
- collecting and evaluating organizations' applications for services based on a registration form developed by the CBI program;
- establishing initial relationships with organization representatives;
- making site visit arrangements, creating timelines, establishing deadlines, and so forth;
- making follow-up telephone calls and liaising with organization representatives;
- writing follow-up correspondence for each NGO;
- arranging initial meetings with NGO representatives and students;
- collecting guests' comments and feedback after a group of students completed a particular project or at the end of all presentations;
- preparing evaluation forms for NGOs;
- contacting NGOs to confirm the format of the certificate;
- helping NGOs evaluate the CBI program; and
- helping students evaluate their peers.

Additional staff activities

Although the lists of activities related to the three primary constituencies are relatively stark itemizations of the kinds of activities in which CBI program team members were engaged, they give some of the flavor of what was going on routinely within the project's daily life. This activity was punctuated with attendance at regional and international conferences, team meetings, leaflet construction, name card design, web site construction, and detailed record keeping. Finally, the staff were very proactive in representing HKBU to share our experiences with our service-learning partners and those who wish to learn from our experience in Southeast Asia and China. Collectively, these kinds of activities seem to have resulted in increased student commitment in the classes served and wider faculty support throughout the university as the semesters unfolded.

Conclusion

The service-learning activities in the CBI program at HKBU focused almost exclusively on finding ways for students to perform academically relevant service as part of a course assignment. The point was to engage students in creative problem solving, to encourage them to take greater responsibility for their own learning, and to develop socially responsible attitudes toward their community. Along the way, we learned several lessons that may be useful to others.

The most significant lesson we learned in operating the kind of service-learning program we designed concerned how labor-intensive it is working with our three primary constituencies: faculty, students and NGOs. Each group initially had to be persuaded to participate and required careful nurturing at every step along the way. Over time, we developed consistent routines and a reservoir of adaptable formats that facilitated the team's work among the various teachers, students, and agencies, which all required extensive time commitments every day. Initial successes and word-of-mouth advertising within all three constituencies made life much easier as the semesters went by and the program grew in numbers of faculty, students, and NGO partners served. Consequently, the second lesson we learned is how beneficial it was to have a small but dedicated full-time staff. For a university to try to implement service-learning broadly throughout the curriculum definitely requires a staff hired specifically for and dedicated to the purpose. For example, as principal supervisor of the project, I still had a full slate of normal faculty duties to perform and could not dedicate myself to the logistics of operating the program every day. The project was only possible because the grant allowed us to hire two people whose only duties were to shepherd the project along, and especially to work with the constituencies.

The third lesson we learned concerned the extensive network of service-learning programs that are available throughout the world. Our initial proposal team was aware to some extent that many people were doing service-learning using many different models (especially in North America), but until we had secured the grant and were actually in operation, we were certainly not aware of the breadth of resources available and the number of people who are willing to contribute their expertise here in the Asia-Pacific region. Of course, we had to search them out initially and that took time, but in the end, the discovery of that rich vein of experience was a revelation for which we are very grateful.

The wealth of available expertise leads to the final lesson that should be featured for those proposing service-learning programs of the type we provided, especially for those seeking institutional (financial) support for their efforts: there is a strong need for service-learning staff to participate in professional conferences as part of their staff development. During our five-year period of operation, our team members had financial support to attend several international conferences on service-learning and were therefore able to tap into the available expertise in a more direct and personal way than simply looking up Internet sites and making email contact. Given the amount of work involved in operating our program, the simple support of making personal human contact periodically to share experiences was a tremendous asset. Such contact was personally encouraging and professionally necessary. In retrospect, I am certain we could not have sustained our year-to-year efforts at the level required for a meaningful program were it not for periodic attendance at conferences with others who were equally committed to the educational goals of service-learning. Thus, when putting together a proposal for service-learning, I am convinced that a small but meaningful part of the budget must be committed to supporting professional development through staff attendance at regional and international service-learning conferences.

At the end of its life as a University Grants Committee supported initiative, the CBI program at HKBU has now become a part of the university's Centre for Holistic Teaching and Learning, where it is currently being developed under new leadership as part of a revised and enlarged educational vision. In this way, the community-based education proposal and grant implementation team has fulfilled its original mission and contributed to what we anticipate will be even better things to come in the development of service-learning at the university.

6 | How Actions Can Become Learning: The Cross-cultural Effectiveness of Service-learning in Asia

Jens Mueller and Dennis Lee

Service-learning has emerged as a powerful tool to teach community-based business concepts to university students. With practical experiences complementing classroom teachings, it is argued that students learn more and understand that sustainable businesses are rooted in their community. Management education has taken note of this shift toward a practice-based approach and has begun to introduce more practitioners as teaching resources, send students outside the university to apply their learning, and let students compete based on measurements not purely academic in nature but related to the practical relevance of their accomplishments (Still and Clayton 2004; Mueller, Thornton, Watt, and Gore 2004).

Resulting from the closer relationship between management schools and businesses, traditional management education has been criticized for lacking reality, while service-learning appears to offer alternatives to classroom teaching (Waddock and Post 2000). Contrary to internship models, where the student appears to be the sole beneficiary, service-learning models introduce students into an external community environment—often with business mentoring added as a connective element—to create a real-world experience, which arguably helps the student develop skills of interest and relevance to future employers. Former HSBC Singapore Chief Executive Officer Paul Lawrence hopes a service-learning program will "help university students in Singapore to expand their skills and outlook, and to prepare themselves for the opportunities presented by businesses in the global economy" (Lawrence 2005, 2).

For this study, we reviewed the quality of service-learning projects engaged in by Asian students in one specific program—Students in Free Enterprise (SIFE)—in several Asian countries. SIFE has operated in more than 45 countries for more than six years. With performance data collected on participants in the same program in several Asian countries, we can offer a cross-border review of service-learning effectiveness. We analyze the learning that has been achieved by those students, and then contrast these results to outcomes from similar service projects in other countries to determine if the learning is dependent on the cultural environment of the students.

Background

The increasing connections between businesses and management schools have challenged universities to develop teaching models that create practical, relevant learning experiences. Although somewhat hindered by conventional accreditation models that find it hard to assess the academic effects of external student activities, service-learning is supported by business leaders throughout Asia, presumably because of the resulting increase in student competencies (Zlotkowski 1998) and the connection to local communities, which often drive sustainable corporate profits (Arney 2006). Santiago Roces, Wal-Mart's president in Korea, expects service-learning students to "make positive progress to build a better world of business" (Roces 2005, 4). Other initiatives are grounded in what some term the "moral decline" of today's college students (Morton and Troppe 1996, 21–32), and given the recent meteoric rise of income opportunities in many Asian countries, a reality check for emerging young managers appears to be quite appropriate. Such efforts are not without resistance from overworked faculty members, citing the lack of operational infrastructure, time to assist students with the service-learning projects, and so forth (Lamb, Swinth, Vinton, and Lee 1998).

Without doubt, service-learning engagements help students develop problem-solving skills (Godfrey, Illes, and Berry 2005). This is primarily due to the absence of pre-formatted solutions and because each situation is unique, in contrast to case competitions or business plan competitions where student work is fictional rather than practical. Even in largely rules-based topic areas such as accounting, service-learning efforts have demonstrated value (Rose, Rose, and Norman 2005) and service-learning activities now appear in structured MBA programs (Wittmer 2004). We suggest that especially in emerging markets, where the content of traditional learning has changed extensively over the past decades (i.e., from state-planned to free market), service-learning can be a complimentary technique that touches many more participants than could be easily reached through existing teaching methods.

Especially in the field of entrepreneurship, many characteristics such as self-confidence, persistence, and high energy levels cannot be acquired easily in the classroom (Miller 1987). SIFE engages students in their communities and provides the opportunity for them to perform in a real environment, overcome market resistance, structure effective programs, measure outcomes, and demonstrate the results to executives.

Cultural differences affect community behavior and thus the approach to service-learning and its effectiveness. Although Germany, the United States, Australia, and New Zealand have been free market countries for all of their existence, business leaders in China and Singapore operate with a strong recognition of political involvement in economic activity and long-term strategic positioning. In countries where free market operations have emerged in the not-too-distant-past, entrepreneurship is likely not yet taught by experienced entrepreneurs, and we suggest that this service/action learning program can complement in-class teaching methods.

Although values in China are changing, and resilience and resourcefulness will continue to elevate entrepreneurs towards success (Liao and Sohmen 2001), some entrepreneurial attributes (i.e., positive response to change, initiative, and profit orientation) appear to be in conflict with Chinese values (Kirby and Ying 1995). More recent work found that a sharp contrast existed between Chinese entrepreneurs and Chinese managers regarding individualism, risk, and openness to change. In some areas, particularly risk tolerance, Chinese entrepreneurs scored higher than their American counterparts (Holt 2000). Equally important, entrepreneurship is on the rise in South Korea, with one out of eleven people working for relatively young companies in 2000 (i.e., firms that were established less than three and a half years ago (Park et al. 2001). We therefore conclude that service-learning as part of entrepreneurial skills development is of great importance in these countries.

Methodology

We reviewed several specific action learning projects that were operated under the guidance of the SIFE rules and thus are comparable in complexity and setup for all of the countries we investigated. We then collected data from participants and their academic mentors as to the learning outcome from 477 (service-learning) SIFE students in Korea, Singapore, China, Australia, New Zealand, Germany, and the United States. Because all of the participants have e-mail and Internet access and a command of basic English, an electronic survey tool was used to collect data. The response rates varied greatly, so our reporting is primarily qualitative rather than statistical.

Project Reports

In Chengdu, China, SIFE students went into the community to establish virtual banks and create small flea markets with products supplied by local business sponsors. The goal was to teach the operation of a market economy to the local community. During this project, children teamed up with their parents to help jump generational barriers and integrate parents into the learning.

In Thailand, SIFE students connected local manufacturers to a network of global buyers to establish sustainable export opportunities. Workshops were held, attended, and supported by local business executives (i.e., from KPMG and HSBC) to teach manufacturers the skills needed to export directly and not through middlemen.

In Australia, SIFE students developed a business support program to teach Australia's aborigines financial planning and business skills to help them conduct business outside their own tribal communities and tap into the value of the mainstream Australian economy.

In Takasaki City, Japan, SIFE students taught community elders how to rejuvenate a cluster of struggling downtown retail shops. Through lessons given by the service-learning students to their elders, contemporary marketing methods were brought into an otherwise closed community, resulting in a vibrant and thriving market area.

Near Whakatane, New Zealand, SIFE students solicited donations of goods and money from local businesses to teach business skills to indigenous Maori by creating a chicken farm. Skills development included team governance to operate the farm, marketing and sales techniques to sell eggs, and networking with the local business community.

Data Review

We reviewed responses from both SIFE students and their academic faculty, with the assumption that the students' self-reporting of skills might be overly flattering as to their contribution to humankind.

SIFE students reported significant enthusiasm for their service-learning projects, often far exceeding the time requirements for traditional classroom academic effort. Students spent an average of more than 15 hours per week on these external activities, clearly indicating their commitment and interest for service-learning. This commitment is so significant that it might raise an issue of time conflicts between service-learning outside of the classroom and commitments to classroom work. We suggest that academic mentors must mitigate adverse impacts on the participants' general learning by managing the time that is committed to service-learning activities.

Students reported uniformly that learning through service had occurred (see Figure 6.1). We note that students can clearly associate learning during their work with specific categories tested in the survey.

Aside from a slightly less enthusiastic affirmation of learning in Singapore and Germany (45% to 55% of the students reported "a lot" of learning, and another 35% to 50% reported "a bit" of learning), of greater interest to academics will be that the specific skills developed through these efforts are not just the traditional tools-based skills of financial analysis, planning, and so forth. The students reported that they had learned teamwork skills, are more proficient in speaking in front of a challenging audience, and are more self-assured. These skills are generally harder to develop in the abstract environment of a university building, and through a faculty that does not always contribute practical commercial experience as their own skill set. We conclude that these learnings are valuable for the participants' development of managerial skills and might improve their employability upon graduation.

To better understand whether their learning was noticeable to outsiders, we asked the students' academic faculty in four countries to affirm skills development. Highly ranked by academics were team building and team management skills, in addition to presentation skills at a professional "real-life" level (Figure 6.2). This testing series was intended to assure that the service-learning outcomes were validated externally through a mentor who could comment on the students' growth throughout the project duration.

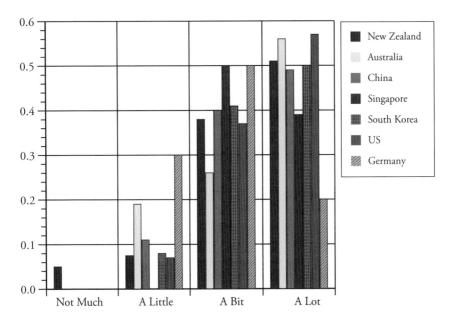

Figure 6.1 To what extent did you learn new skills?

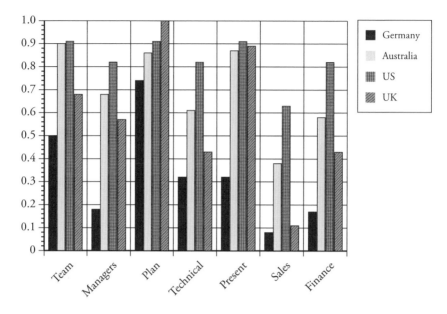

Figure 6.2 What skills did the students learn? (Faculty opinion)

Conclusion

As a result of investigating the service-learning effort of SIFE students in seven countries on three continents, we found that there are no significant cultural-based variations of outcomes. Although the sophistication of service-learning projects vary greatly among countries (e.g., projects are more highly developed and complex in the United States, Australia, and New Zealand) to take into account the community's needs, the learning outcomes were uniform for the student participants. Intangible skills such as leadership, teamwork, networking, and sensitivity to community needs ranked highly in the list of achievements by service-learning students, and we speculate that those skills are as relevant to future employers as they are hard to teach in the traditional teaching environment of a classroom.

This service-learning approach requires input and guidance from faculty, staff, and external business people, and thus can be internally complex. We note, however, that the learning achieved — aside from the community benefits extended through the knowledge transferred by participants — is significant and complementary to those usually imparted during formal in-class teachings.

7 Intercultural Service-learning and Multicultural Symbiosis

Enrique G. Oracion

Service-learning as a pedagogy brings students to the community not only to serve, but also to learn as they work within the limits of capabilities and resources with locals (Oracion 2002, OSL 2006). As a form of experiential learning, it helps students value their education and discover their potential to be change agents while still in school. It offers them opportunities to become creative participants in the learning process because of the relative independence they have from their teachers when they are entrusted to a community or agency (McCarthy 2007b, 8). They are not in constant contact with their teachers for guidance or immediate answers to questions. Their community exposure brings them to a different world of learning experiences where there are no formalities, examinations, comfortable chairs, and tables at which they can write and conduct experiments.

Beyond the walls of the classroom and the gates of the schools are realities that may be totally new to students, especially those who live in gated communities (i.e., expensive subdivisions and condominiums) and in the comfort of their families (Oracion 2006). The opening of physical barriers through service-learning puts students in different social and cultural milieus where they must adapt in order to effectively experience the different and varied worlds of human struggle and existence. McCarthy (2007b, 13) suggests that service-learning moves students out of their "familiar comfort zones" and poses "new challenges, but also new successes for them." It is presumed that any student will initially experience cultural shock and how they regard it depends on their inherent or learned ability to overcome it, in either a painful or easy way. It is expected that students' personal growth, self-fulfillment, and satisfaction will be enhanced by the end of their service-learning involvement (OSL 2006, 9).

For international students or those who come to serve and learn in a foreign host country, being part of an intercultural service-learning program not only introduces them to a community where they are in a close encounter with another culture, it also puts them into intimate contact with students from diverse and contrasting cultural backgrounds (McCarthy 2007a). Therefore, students must engage with two levels of cultural adjustments in order to meaningfully achieve their goals in joining the program; that is, they must adjust to their host communities and fellow students. They must strive to overcome their ethnocentricity and begin to comprehend the reality of living in the host community from the perspective of locals, a major step to achieving cultural relativity (Benderly et al. 1977, 15). Adjusting to an unfamiliar culture, or not, is a measure of their flexibility, for now and perhaps in the future. Students can begin to see their own cultures "from different angles and stop taking them for granted" and "begin to understand that cultural differences are products of their own environment and conditions, their existence relative to their context" (Nishio 2007, 26).

Multicultural Symbiosis

Ecologically, symbiosis refers to a mutually beneficial relationship among organisms (Scaff 1982, 73). When applied to human interaction amidst cultural diversity, the concept of *multicultural symbiosis* implies how the coming together of people with diverse cultural backgrounds offers relative benefits to all involved. It reflects the idea that in cultural diversity each person has something to contribute to human survival, which is similar to biological diversity (Milton 1996, 140). In contrast to the competition and conflict that often erupt when two or more groups exploit the same habitat, multicultural symbiosis instead transforms these social processes into driving forces for promoting harmonious working relationships or mutual dependence—an argument that can be traced back to systems theory (Duke 1983, 347). It is by appreciating and learning from differences that common goals and cooperation may be realized (Aronson 1997, 342).

Multicultural symbiosis, or *kyosei* in Japanese (i.e., "living together"), served as the theme of the International Service-Learning Model Program (ISLMP) because of the cultural mix of its participants (McCarthy 2007a, 33; Nishio 2007, 26). This was initiated by the International Christian University (ICU) through a grant from the Ministry of Education of Japan and participated in by six schools that are members of the Service-Learning Asia Network (SLAN), which was organized in 2004. These schools were ICU (Japan), Silliman University (Philippines), Lady Doak College (India), Chung Chi College, the

Chinese University of Hong Kong (Hong Kong), Seoul Women's University (South Korea), and Soochow University (Taiwan). Silliman University hosted the ISLMP in August 2006 with 20 student-participants ranging from 19 to 23 years old. They included Filipino (8), Japanese (6), Hong Kong Chinese (2), Korean (2), Taiwanese (1), and Indian (1) students. There were only 2 Filipino males and 2 Japanese males in the group.

The non-Filipino students were from various academic disciplines, backgrounds, and college class levels, while the Filipino students were all majoring in social work, graduating from college, and beginning a one-semester course in community work. The non-Filipino students (except for the Indian student) were on a semester break that freed them from classes to come to the Philippines for the ISLMP. Therefore, the participation of Filipino students in the program was part of their course curriculum while the non-Filipino students earned academic credits, either elective or required, for taking part in the international service-learning program. Their majors included social science (3), social work (2), international studies (1), international relations (1), English literature (1), geography (1), political science (1), communication (1), and mathematics (1).

The 2006 ISLMP was guided by the philosophy that by forging a common purpose of serving communities and learning, intercultural cooperation can be achieved. Learning through service would be advantageous not only to Filipino and other Asian students, but also to the host agencies or communities where the students worked or served. The program's goal was that at the end of the students' community engagement, their experience would reveal to them that serving the community can enhance academic training and vice versa. In other words, they would have experienced a form of reciprocal learning (McCarthy 2007a, 34). They would also appreciate their capacity to help in various community activities and have demonstrated efforts to serve people unknown to them. Ultimately, it was hoped that despite the students' cultural diversity, they would value common social goals and would have made concerted efforts to serve and learn together.

An orientation conducted by the teacher-facilitators and resource persons about the philosophy of the ISLMP and its objectives, Philippine culture and society, and the nature of the communities where students were assigned was found necessary to prepare students for actual community work. The orientation informed students about what was expected of them during and after the program, particularly how they would be evaluated using various indicators. It also prepared them for what they encountered in their respective host communities. Moreover, the students were given a sense of direction and a feeling of being important participants of the program as co-servers and co-learners in a global community.

The students were asked during the orientation about their joys, hopes, and fears about going into communities new to them. Their joys included being able to serve the community where they would be assigned, using what they learned in school, and meeting and making friends with people from different cultures. Related to these joys, they hoped that they could successfully extend services and make a difference in the lives of others and similarly provide them with new experiences. However, they feared that they would fail to effectively relate with others due to cultural differences and be unable to extend services because of the gaps this may create. A number also feared getting sick or had concerns about their safety in places unfamiliar to them. These sentiments were processed during the orientation and the students were given tips on how to cope with their fears and to achieve what they hoped for when serving the community.

The students were divided into eight groups for their community engagement, composed of two to three members each (with one Filipino student in each group), corresponding to the number of host communities to which they were assigned. They were randomly assigned to these communities, which were spread geographically and economically. Three are "built" communities in Dumaguete City—housing projects for indigent and resettled families. Three communities are situated along the coast and two are upland villages between 8 and 60 kilometers from Dumaguete City. These are farming and fishing communities. The students lived and served in these communities for a total of 15 days. They went back to Silliman University on weekends for needed breaks from community work and for their reflection sessions about how they experienced multicultural symbiosis. The composition of students and their community assignments had indeed tested the concept of multicultural symbiosis.

The succeeding sections discuss how the students demonstrated the essence of service-learning and multicultural symbiosis during and at the end of their community engagement. Data for the study came from the report of the 2006 ISLMP at Silliman University—a compilation of the proceedings of the orientation program, discussions during the weekly reflection sessions, and the analysis of the quantitative and qualitative assessments of students about their experiences in the program (Silliman University 2006).

Forms of Service: Being Generalists in Response to Opportunities

It is ideal to fit the skills of students engaged in service-learning to the needs of existing projects of host agencies in certain communities (e.g., OSL 2006).

Failure to do so may frustrate the students when they feel they have nothing to contribute to community well-being. They may think that their academic preparation lags far behind the overwhelming needs of the community, but in community-based service-learning, students have to discover the ways in which they can best serve the locals. It takes time, but is more fulfilling at the end, when they experience being able to serve in their own limited ways. This was the case of a group of the ISLMP students who said they found the problems of the community where they were assigned too complex and they did not have the power to solve them. They were disappointed and confused at first. These sentiments are perhaps reflections of the idealism of young students who want to be of service to others, and especially for those who are first-timers in community work.

Another group of students said they thought there would be activities lined up for them according to their skills, but instead they had to plan their own activities. As the students became immersed with the community, they eventually discovered that there were a variety of needs and activities where they could be useful. They became creative in developing ways to be of service to the families that hosted them or to the community where they resided for the duration of the program. They learned to fit their skills to available opportunities or community needs, particularly those within their capabilities and talents. They also had to learn new skills in order to maximize the ways in which they could be involved in community activities.

In general, the students of the 2006 ISLMP can be considered as generalists rather than specialists in terms of the services they rendered. They were learners who wished to contribute to community life and learn in the process, so the amount and quality of service they rendered cannot be judged according to the standards used for professional community or extension workers. A particular batch of students serving a community cannot yield a significant impact unless the community hosts different batches of service-learning students over a longer period of time. This issue was brought up in the first reflection session, and the recognition helped students psychologically. Nevertheless, after a week in the community, a female non-Filipino student noted, "If I open my mind I can do more than I thought."

Although they were treated initially as guests by their respective host families, a gesture usually extended by Filipinos to new acquaintances who stay with them, the students were eventually given their share of domestic tasks. According to the host families, they were not required to do the tasks; rather, the students volunteered. For non-Filipino students, many of these tasks were new to them, but they enjoyed doing them because they learned what everyday life is like in another culture. Preparing meals, marketing, washing dishes, and keeping surroundings clean are universal activities, but the manner in which these are done varies from culture to culture. The students also participated in community service that benefited certain groups or the community as a whole. For example, some students tutored children in mathematics and English. Despite how small the services extended were, one group of students believed that their activities had helped a lot.

Other examples of activities that made an impact within the communities included working together with the locals to clean and beautify, and preparing herbal medicines introduced by the student nurses of Silliman University. These activities helped to promote proper sanitation and provide the community with a local supply of affordable alternative medicines. The students also helped bake native bread; participated in beach seine fishing; helped make candles, ice-cream, and concrete pavers; contributed labor toward gardening and producing coconut virgin oil; and assisted in cleaning and splitting bamboos for making functional items. These activities added to household or cooperative income while teaching ISLMP students how difficult making a living can be in the community, due to the limited capital and resources of its residents.

Unlike their counterparts, when their initial and final community engagements were compared, the Filipino students reported that their involvement in the economic activities of their host families and communities had significantly improved. Although all students observed, analyzed, and planned their involvement in the community's economy during the first week, the Filipino students were more accustomed to the local way of life and so they got more involved in what the locals were doing for a living. However, they had to overcome the community's incorrect impressions about why they were there. A Filipino student said, "the community thought that our purpose of going there is to give money because I am with two foreigners." When the students explained that they were there to serve and work with them rather than to give them money, the inaccurate perception eventually disappeared.

Meaning of Service: Altruism in the Making

Service in a service-learning program means extending help or sharing skills and talents for the benefit of people who are strangers to the students. It is pro-social behavior, but short of altruism, because the latter means helping others without any expectation of return (Aronson et al. 1997, 406). Service-learning may be less or not at all altruistic because of the learning or the grade the students expect to earn in exchange, or the joy they experience from having helped, but eventually it helps students develop empathy — a feeling that precedes the desire to serve others. When one can feel the pain, the need, and the struggle of another, he or she will help regardless of the gain (Aronson et al. 1997, 406). That is why a volunteer service program is being designed at Silliman University to respond to those students who wish to continue in community service after having completed the course-related service-learning program.

It is hoped that service-learning students will have internalized the meaning of real service to others by the time they graduate from college. One Filipino social work student said during the reflection session that because of this exposure, "I understood more the role of the social worker in giving service and welfare to the people." In a synthesis of their experiences in community service during the reflection session, the following related sentiments are evident: a desire to deepen value of service or selflessness; expressions of dedication or love for everything they did; and commitment and sensitivity to the needs of others. Furthermore, service-learning gave them a greater sense of ownership of what they had done for the community. It gave them self-confidence in their ability to do what they believed they could despite their inherent limitations. All types of students experienced significant improvements in the ideas and activities that they themselves conceived, developed, and eventually introduced to the community. Because there were no major pre-designed activities waiting for service-learning students when they entered into their respective host communities, it logically follows that they would claim to have introduced their ideas and activities as forms of community service. The services rendered by students indicate their creativity and sensitivity in responding to the community's needs after consulting with the locals.

What the students expressed or demonstrated about how they served the host communities were confirmed by the assessments done by their respective host families at the end of the program. They wrote that the students expressed joy for having helped others, especially the children. The students showed willingness and readiness to be involved in several community activities, suggested worthwhile activities, clarified what needed to be done when they did not understand it, and were conscientious and cautious about their schedule in accomplishing assigned tasks. Host families thought the students were friendly, observant, and intelligent because they easily dealt with the locals and were empathetic to the circumstances in the community.

Teamwork: Producing Results with Common Vision

During the 2006 ISLMP, working groups were composed of students of different nationalities, and a Filipino student was assigned to serve as direct link to its host community. Even though they were culturally diverse, each group performed as a team. During the reflection sessions, when the students shared experiences, it was apparent that they deliberately planned their daily activities as a team. They jointly made decisions and implemented their plans together. An example of how students planned their initial and subsequent activities included their decision to begin by interviewing the village officials and the residents about the condition of the community, and doing it together as a team. Their host families said they had observed them doing the interviews.

As the weeks passed while working together in the community, one student in an all-female group recalled that "our relationship had improved; there [was] mutual support and cooperation between us." She went on to say that "we became closer because we were sharing our personal things like perfume, skin lotion. We felt like sisters, like relatives." Some female students also shared beds. The relationship as co-learners was elevated to a more personalized level where inhibitions were erased and the real personalities of students surfaced. However, it was not always that easy, because at times tensions erupted among members of the group when cultural and personal differences unavoidably clashed. During the reflection sessions, the teacher-facilitators came in to settle misunderstandings before the problem became worse. Thus, for service-learning programs to be successful, the importance of teacher-facilitators and the holding of regular reflection sessions cannot be denied (McCarthy 2007b, 13).

Teamwork is always a product of group effort and is not unilaterally created; it is negotiated to become a mutually beneficial engagement. It will not effectively work when members of the group hesitate to submit to the majority's will. Mutual understanding and the recognition that each member of the group has something to contribute are basic requirements for achieving teamwork. Regarding the notion about how friendship precedes teamwork, a student described what kept them going as a group: "The important thing is that we know our weaknesses, to be open-minded, and to understand the reasons behind some actions, and not to question right away what the other teammate is doing even if contrary to my values. This has kept the friendship going." The students in one group pointed out that "our relationship became better because we have the same likes." Another said that "both of us [were] afraid of seeing a corpse, but we just [went] and visit the bereaved family and hold [held] hands." Comforting each other brought them closer.

Forms of Learning: Personal Skills, Values and Social Sensitivity

If the students are passive and hesitant to aggressively interact with the community, less can be achieved by the end of the program. As mentioned, students spent the first week of community engagement interviewing locals and "hanging around" the neighborhood, observing what people were doing and participating in their activities. Through directly and indirectly soliciting information, they were able to decide what services to undertake that would help their host communities. This was evident during the first reflection session when the students were reporting about the conditions of their respective host communities.

Aside from building teamwork, the other skill students learned was how to become inquisitive and observant about the community and the people they met daily. Their host families confirmed their acquisition of this skill in their assessment of the students. It was in living with poor families, engaging in casual conversations and home visitations, and hanging around that the students had close and personal encounters with the realities confronting the poor—realities that significantly contrasted with those enjoyed by the students, especially those from industrialized Asian countries. For example, two groups discovered during home visits the sad conditions of a battered wife, a baby suffering from a heart ailment, and a mentally disturbed woman they believed must be helped. They referred these cases to local government social workers for assistance or interventions. In these instances, they learned to mediate between people in need and an appropriate helping agency.

Students also noticed that despite the poverty commonly seen among households in their host communities, Filipinos are still happy and close to every family member. They observed school children who came to school late because they must walk three to four hours before reaching school. Some pupils had to cross rivers several times, which made it difficult to go to school during bad weather. Teachers told the students that some of their pupils came to class without having breakfast. This awakened the non-Filipino students who have opportunities to earn a quality education. One student was impressed with the sacrifices made by Filipino children to enable them to attend school. Another said, "The fact that the children go to school despite the long hours of walking is a manifestation that they are interested in pursuing their education." A non-Filipino student better appreciated what she has and was grateful to her "environment back home." In the same vein, a Filipino student said, "I am very thankful that my parents send me to [a] school like . . . Silliman University." The students all said they valued what God has given them.

Meanwhile, attending the lavish birthday party of a local politician and comparing it to the poverty they saw being experienced by many in the community raised the issue of social disparity. Similarly, students assigned in different communities saw the way families work to secure basic needs, to provide for the medical needs of sick family members, or to send children to school with their meager income. A female non-Filipino student was sad despite the festive mood of that birthday party because of the contrast — a feeling made

100 Enrique G. Oracion

worse when she thought about how she could not help, as a student, to solve the problem of social inequity. What the students were doing for the community may have no direct impact in solving the poverty people had been suffering for many years, but the students' concern and willingness to help, as one host family described it, served as an inspiration to locals to continue their struggle. This example shows how direct community engagement had contributed to the social sensitivity of ISLMP students.

Students also learned patience. This was particularly true for those who were teaching or tutoring school children, especially the non-Filipino — not only because it was a first experience for them but also due to language barriers. They observed behavioral problems inside the classroom, which requires a patient and understanding teacher. But more than that, they saw a bleak future for these children if this behavior continued without being mitigated. They attributed this problem to the school setting, which is evident in the group's reflection:

> The elementary school (classroom) is very hot. How can students study in a hot environment? The classroom has only one wall fan and it was not working . . . Some pupils always go out, not listening to the teacher. If the pupils cannot continue with their education, they will not prosper. And this will continue from one generation to another . . .

This statement further points out how much value the ISLMP students put on education as a vehicle for social mobility. The contrasting pictures they saw between the degree holders in urban centers and the poor people in the community must have led them to such a conclusion.

In sum, when their experiences during their initial and post-engagement with the community were compared, degrees of improvement can be observed regarding what the students knew about the life stories of the host communities and the locals. However, this improvement is more significantly seen in the case of non-Filipino students, because they were complete outsiders to the community. This is also true in terms of the students realizing their personal goals and social roles, and in learning new things not taught in the classroom. Overall, this implies that time plays an important role in students understanding their host communities and effectively relating and working with the locals.

Interestingly, Filipino students learned more about the strengths and weaknesses of their host communities, and they became more aware of their own personal strengths and limitations. Such congruence indicates how able the Filipino students were to see themselves in relation to the communities where they were assigned. Furthermore, unlike the non-Filipino students, the Filipinos learned to be more independent in caring for themselves, perhaps because of their assigned task of looking after their non-Filipino partners.

Reaction to Others: Navigating Differences

As previously mentioned, students had to culturally navigate relationships with their fellow students and the communities where they were assigned. This was not easy to do, particularly by non-Filipino students, who had to also overcome language barriers. Nonetheless, many among the less schooled Filipinos can speak and understand a little English because of the American occupation of their country. English is used in school instruction and in the mass media, particularly television and foreign movies (in digital format) that reach as far as the remotest villages where there is electricity. Consequently, even if the non-Filipino students did not speak English well, it served as a medium of communication between them and the community. One student said, "In Taiwan, we don't speak English. [I'm] not very good in English. [But] I was able to overcome my fears in communicating in English."

However, in one instance, a non-Filipino student felt left out because her Filipino partner and the locals usually spoke in the local dialect when they talked to each other. She also complained that her host parents, who felt awkward about their English, did not often talk to her, although they treated her well. This is in contrast with the host family of another group of students who was fluent in English; they easily understood each other. Indeed, the ability to communicate in whatever language is understood by the parties involved is a primary consideration for ultimately enabling intercultural interaction to be mutually advantageous. Communication through a common language holds a group together, because most ideas and knowledge are transmitted by using it, according to anthropologists (Benderly et al. 1977, 55). However, given more time in the community and a willingness to learn the dialect would allow the non-Filipino students to communicate with the locals.

Nevertheless, there are always means by which outsiders can penetrate the inner circle of a group or community. Some host families noticed that the non-Filipino students were trying to learn the dialect in talking with the locals. Meanwhile, other non-Filipinos communicated with the children by playing games with them and teaching them origami (the Japanese art of paper folding) and songs. Others also pro-actively looked for ways to be involved in household tasks so they could interact with members of the family, even with the use of sign language. Therefore, it was also by engaging in activities where there was a commonality of interest and a source of joy or comfort that they learned to get along well. As a consequence, this helped non-Filipino students develop greater understanding about the locals compared to the Filipino students. Filipino students took many things about the locals for granted because they seemed ordinary due to their cultural heritage.

It was the first time for many of the non-Filipino students to stay in the homes of poor families for a length of time, but how they were treated significantly helped them to make the necessary adjustments. For example, one student reported, "My host family treated me as a real family member and I felt very comfortable there." This sentiment illustrates the important role host families play in community-based service-learning programs. For this reason, the host families were oriented to the program before the students were sent to live with them. Because the arrival of students would disrupt the host families' normal life, they also had to make some adjustments. Nonetheless, their acceptance of hosting the students in their homes indicated their capacity to adjust. In order not to burden them, they were given money to buy the food they served to students who stayed with them.

Students had to be ready for any eventuality and resilient in the face of whatever circumstances arose. One student considered preparedness important in responding to the demands of a certain time and place. Information about cultural diversity and potential necessary adjustments passed along by teacher-facilitators helped students to understand the particular behavior of their partners and the locals rather than being disillusioned. For example, being unaware of the circumstances, outsiders may stereotype and make harsh judgments when community residents appear lazy. Some non-Filipino students characterized the people in the community where they were assigned as lazy, which they attributed to the prevalence of poverty. They observed that many appeared idle most of the time and, therefore, according to their standards time was wasted. Understandably, they had this impression because they were raised in big cities where people are always busy making a living. Correspondingly, the fast pace of non-Filipino students drew negative comments from Filipino students: "They are always on the move and want things immediately done." This behavior caused some of them to earn the stereotypes of being pushy and insensitive. Conversely, one student commented that Filipinos always have the time to relax, especially after lunch, thus describing the Filipinos' easy-going behavior or their tendency to take matters lightly. During the reflection session, the teacher-facilitators explained to the non-Filipino students the seeming "laziness" of the locals, emphasizing that the context should be considered before making judgments. With reference to the residents of an urban housing project for the poor, one teacher-facilitator explained that "there are always people sitting down, seemingly wasting time, but actually they are regaining their energy because some of them are working in the port area as stevedores, even until night time." This is in addition to the fact that there are only a limited number of jobs available for them, which means things may be different when there are more available employment opportunities. Meanwhile, many people in the rural areas usually rested and talked with friends over *tuba* (coconut toddy) after they arrived from their farms. A teacher-facilitator explained that they normally go to their farms very early in the morning and come home when it is hot, so climate is also a very important factor to consider.

In contrast to what others thought, a non-Filipino student who better understood the behavior of Filipinos did not think that the residents in her host community were lazy. Another non-Filipino student believed that certain social norms in the community cannot be changed in so short a time, even if cultural practices are negative or do not contribute to the well-being of Filipino families. Furthermore, one cannot just impose his or her values; the locals have to be respected, the student observed.

Tensions usually erupt when differences cannot be reconciled. This can happen when being different is not acceptable to either party or one is unwilling to change even when necessary. But the ISLMP students must have successfully overcome cultural stereotypes and understood why cultural differences exist, because at the end of their community engagement they positively rated their experiences regarding cultural relations. All the students reported experiencing significant improvements in their ability to relate with other students and to understand the locals amidst the cultural differences that at first prevented them from appreciating each other. Such intimacy is evident in the statement of a Japanese student: "I really felt I am a member of the community. I will really miss my [host] community." In fact, after she returned home, she immediately applied for and was accepted to the ICU-SU student exchange program so she could return. She often visited her former host community while studying at Silliman University.

How much the service-learning experiences of students impacted their relationships with partner students and host families became more evident during the closing program when a farewell dinner was held for non-Filipino students. The impressions shared by representatives from each group of students revealed that they deeply valued the friendships they had forged with their partner students and host families while living and working together in the community. Gifts were exchanged between Filipino and non-Filipino students and students gave gifts to the host families as tokens of gratitude. The gifts' value was assessed not just for their material worth, but more importantly, as symbols of multicultural symbiosis or mutual cooperation that the ISLMP experience facilitated despite the short period of intercultural contact. Numerous emotions were expressed at the farewell dinner, and tears fell when students said goodbye to their respective host families and the Filipino students. Cameras captured memorable moments of hugging and kissing as they took leave of those they had begun to understand, appreciate, and love. It is when one has touched the lives of others in some way, even for a short period of time, that bidding goodbye seems to take time. The non-Filipino students must have realized that entering a community may be difficult because of some apprehensions or fears, but it was difficult to leave when they had learned to love it. The emotional exchanges of goodbyes continued the next day in the Dumaguete Airport when the Filipino students, along with some host families, sent the non-Filipino students off.

Beyond Service-learning: Student Reflections on the Future

The impact of intercultural service-learning on students can be gauged not only by the knowledge and skills they learned but also how it influences their direction in life or what they would like to do in the future. Students said it helped them examine their personal lives and home countries by comparing or contrasting them with what they observed and learned from their host communities. This must have been more significantly felt by non-Filipino students, particularly the Japanese. For example, Japanese students developed the ability to correct or clarify what actually happened in the history of their country in relation to neighboring Asian countries during World War II (see also McCarthy 2007a, 36). They wished to prevent the recurrence of past negative events and to further improve present diplomatic relationships. It is in this area that intercultural service-learning achieves multicultural symbiosis at a higher level.

Based on the results of the reflection sessions, other things may occur during and after the ISLMP experience, particularly to non-Filipino students. Once they return home, they can preserve the practices or traits they found to be working well in their host communities. Examples of these traits are the closeness of family and community relationships, contentment, and having time to relax and being happy amidst problems — Filipino traits that contrast with the fast pace of life and materialism that seem to prevail in most industrialized countries. In addition, they better appreciate what they have that their host communities do not enjoy, such as relative abundance and convenience in their daily lives. Moreover, their ISLMP experience can help them think about ways in which their own countries can help improve the social, economic, and political situations in the Asian regions.

The ISLMP gave students a greater sense of meaning about what they can or will do to be of service to others. A Taiwanese student considered her experience in the program to have solidified her dream of becoming a missionary doctor. In particular, her encounter with a baby suffering from a congenital heart problem made her think that she should definitely pursue a medical degree because she would like to operate on the baby for free. Of course, this may be more an indication of the empathy she gained, because becoming a medical doctor would take many years to realize and by that time the baby may be gone. Nevertheless, it was an expression of concern for the disadvantaged compared to the kind of life she enjoys and the amount of resources she has at home.

The Taiwanese student was not the only one who had these kinds of feelings. All the other students expressed greater desire to share whatever resources and skills they have with other communities in the future. They believed that the ISLMP had bolstered their preparation toward becoming successful practitioners in the careers they were pursuing. More specifically, the Filipino students reported to have increased their desire to engage in community work in other courses to add more to what they learned from their ISLMP experience. This is expected, because social work students will ultimately be working with communities as professionals. Interestingly, the non-Filipino students, as complete outsiders, had equally demonstrated their flexibility and creativity in learning new skills in order to be of service to their host communities.

Moving Forward: Achievements and Lessons Learned

What did we, as an academic institution, learn about organizing the ISLMP? Primarily, it informed us that, because it cuts across cultures, it not only tests students' abilities to render service given their inherent limitations in terms of skills and material resources, but also their adaptability to cultural behavioral differences and to the inconvenience they must experience due to the socioeconomic differences between them and their host communities. It also demonstrates that the students as a group can successfully work or serve the community despite the differences in their academic training if they are highly motivated and adequately oriented to what is expected of them. In fact, the ISLMP students demonstrated willingness to serve given their limitations and their ability to learn under whatever circumstances occur—qualities they need in facing the real world after they graduate from college.

Secondly, the program proves the need for the teacher-facilitators and the students to deliberately plan how the different aspects of the program's implementation (i.e., orientation, immersion, community service, reflection session, and evaluation or assessment) should be conducted. The orientation is important because it is when students are informed about the specific objectives and schedules of the program, prepared psychologically to adapt to personality and cultural differences (e.g., language, religion, food preferences, personal hygiene), and guided in how to accomplish teamwork with fellow students and the locals. It is in immersion that the students are expected to apply the guidelines given to them in their orientation and to initiate ways by which they will know more about their partner students and their host families and communities so that they can effectively engage in community service.

In community service, the students are expected to exercise what they learned in class or to learn new things with their partner students and the locals so they can work well together. However, it may be a different situation when students are working with agencies that have already prepared certain tasks for them that are appropriate to their skills. If there are no specific activities prepared for students, what they learn during community immersion is helpful in planning how they can best serve the host communities. Meanwhile, during the weekend reflection sessions, the students engage in self-examination with regard to what they did and learned during community service. Their reflections should go beyond the knowledge they gained; it should also cover what service to others means to them and the values they attached to what they have shared (e.g., McCarthy 2007b, 13).

The evaluation or assessment of the impact of service-learning, an important activity that measures the results of the program, should be done after the students' initial community engagement in order to establish baseline data to compare with the data generated at the terminal stage. Data gathering can be done in several ways, depending on the goals of the program and the domains it wants to measure. It may use any or a combination of different sources of data, such as the content of the students' daily journals or qualitative self-assessment, synthesis of the reflection sessions, students' quantitative self-ratings, and the teacher-facilitator, host family, or agency assessments. It may measure its impact on the student, community, agency, or school, and be done objectively or subjectively based on certain variables. In this chapter, the focus is only on the impacts of the ISLMP on students using self-assessment and the evaluation of host communities.

Finally, the ISLMP was the first to test the variables in measuring the impacts of service-learning introduced during a conference in Hong Kong on "Service-Learning Evaluation Strategies and Program Assessment" sponsored by the United Board for Christian Higher Education in Asia (Abregana 2006). The variables include awareness of community, involvement with community, commitment in service, career choices, self-awareness, personal development, academic achievement, sensitivity to diversity, autonomy and independence, sense of ownership, and communication. These variables specifically measure how much students gained after their community engagement in terms of relating with the community, valuing themselves and other people, applying learned skills, and acquiring new knowledge.

Certain aspects in the implementation of the ISLMP as hosted by Silliman University need some improvements as it pursues community-based service-learning programs—issues and lessons that may apply to other universities. Letting non-Filipino students live in host communities in the Philippines for a longer period of time so they could have greater impact is financially costly for them. Therefore, Silliman University Service-Learning Program must establish a continuing partnership with host communities to identify projects where students can immediately be assigned. This actually echoes the suggestion of host communities that the students have a longer time period or more days for actual community service. In effect, the impact of the program on the community would be more significantly felt because the services rendered by a group of students would not be limited to a particular period of time. Instead, there could be continuity among groups of students as they serve the same host community.

Projects must be appropriate to the needs of the communities and should be identified together with the locals during the planning stage in forging a partnership for service-learning. These may revolve around livelihood, health and nutrition, literacy, and related concerns, and should be coordinated with the university's extension program. Livelihood projects were primarily suggested by the host communities because of the unemployment problem that was common in all the communities where the ISLMP students were assigned. Community leaders hoped that some learning materials would be donated to their schools to improve the ability of their children to learn. Such materials could be useful to the ISLMP students who would want to assist teachers in teaching as their community assignment. Students can solicit used books, magazines, and other learning materials as part of their community service. The lesson is that a university's extension program cannot sustain its service-learning program in particular communities unless it decides to work with the existing programs of non-government organizations.

Universities sending students to participate in the ISLMP must always be informed beforehand about the arrangements and mechanics of the community-based service-learning at Silliman University so they can select appropriately the students they will send based on academic preparation and the subjects where students' service-learning outputs can be credited. Community-based service-learning demands that students live with their host families in the communities where they will be assigned and students should be aware of this. The comfort of air-conditioned bedrooms, the soothing baths with running hot and cold water in clean bathrooms, the savor of favored food at home or in restaurants, and many other privileges in the urban world are temporarily denied to them if they really want to immerse themselves in the realities of Filipino rural communities. More importantly, knowing about the host country or community allows students to make informed decisions about accepting the challenge, and prepares them to make necessary cultural adjustments. The students' safety and the benefits that await them must guide their decisions. These are major ethical considerations in intercultural service-learning.

Since students must earn credits for their service-learning involvement, sending universities must make arrangements with Silliman University regarding the requirements they expect to be met by their respective students. However, it must be remembered that the students cannot be evaluated in terms of the impact of the services they rendered to the community (e.g., increase in the income of the community, improvement of the nutritional status of children, ability of children to read and write) because of their limitations in terms of time and resources. Rather, the students should be evaluated on the learning they gained relative to concepts and theories discussed in class. What they learned is evident in their journals, in their sharing during reflection sessions, or in changes of behavior as observed by their teachers before and after service-learning. No matter what procedures are used, the students should always be made aware of how they will be graded, which is another important ethical consideration in service-learning.

Conclusion

Multicultural symbiosis through service-learning can be achieved in the long run if the ISLMP will be sustained by the member institutions of SLAN. There are good reasons to continue this program based on the results of the students' self-assessments and the host community representatives who directly worked with them. The program demonstrates that students can develop ways to be of service to others and to learn in the process. Students felt significant changes regarding their perspectives in life after being exposed to the various realities of their host communities.

The changes within each student are evident in their self-ratings about how service-learning enhanced their values and commitment to community service; reinforced their future careers, goals, and social roles; promoted their sensitivity and adaptability to cultural diversity and new situations; taught them to appreciate learning outside of class; encouraged them to be independent and creative in helping others; and developed their ability to communicate with and understand different individuals. These are all necessary ingredients to attain multicultural symbiosis.

Interestingly, the students said they experienced these changes despite the limited skills, resources, and time they had for their community engagement. Even with these limitations, the host communities still appreciated the students' gestures in serving more than what they actually achieved. Because of the aforementioned limitations, it is perhaps too assuming to say that the 2006 ISLMP has produced these remarkable impacts on students. However, these students cannot altogether fake their experiences and self-assessments to please the individuals behind the program. Thus, it is safe to conclude at this point that there were positive results of the ISLMP as experienced by the students and observed by their host families.

8 | Service-learning in University Curricula: A Case Study at Fu Jen Catholic University

Jen-Chi Yen and Bai-Chuan Yang

Due to the emerging needs and incentives provided by the government, service-learning has become a popular pedagogy in Taiwan. Aside from Fu Jen Catholic University, 86 of the 146 universities and colleges in Taiwan have incorporated service-learning as an essential part of the curriculum. Some of these institutions facilitate service-learning through administrative offices, such as the offices of student affairs and academic affairs, some implement a mentoring system to facilitate service-learning, while others have established a specialized service-learning center to promote service-learning curricula and related programs. The content of the service-learning programs varies widely. Some programs incorporate participation in campus life and community service, while others combine volunteer work and service or professional training.

In May 2007, the Ministry of Education (MOE) in Taiwan officially instituted the Service-Learning Project for Colleges and Universities to encourage students' participation and engagement in social service as a way to foster a sense of responsibility and enhance the qualifications of our future citizens. The MOE plans to incorporate service-learning programs into the regular accreditation of the Annual Teaching Excellence Project funded by the government. Items to be accredited and reviewed include organizational functionality, curriculum planning, teacher profiles, promotional schemes, and course evaluation and award systems. With the active involvement of the MOE, service-learning activities which used to be limited to a small number of universities (particularly those affiliated with religious groups) in Taiwan have become popular among an increasing number of university campuses. More universities are committed to exploring service-learning as pedagogy, developing course materials, and compiling guidelines and procedures in the practice of service-learning. The overall impact of service-learning programs is noticeable among students, the university campus, social agencies, and non-government organizations, and the role of service-learning is expected to increase as more universities become engaged.

Fu Jen started service-learning about a decade ago. Born from the heart of the Church and rooted in the Jesuit educational philosophy, we hope to provide students with an education that features a balanced combination of experience, self-reflection and love. Our persistent efforts to promote service-learning have been one of the ways to fulfill our mission and have been well rewarded. More importantly, its influence has started to spread into various spheres of the community. Now that the policy has officially been implemented at the university, the comprehensive service-learning program has matured and is a model for other universities in Taiwan. The experiences at Fu Jen have been a valuable resource for our counterparts, and the various activities and programs designed for service-learning are worthy lessons for universities interested in developing similar programs.

Implementing a service-learning program was undertaken by Fu Jen to realize its educational goal of fostering each of our students into a "whole person." Through years of experiences, trials, and errors, we have concluded that the most effective model for a service-learning curriculum is one that combines professional training and service. With the guidance of professors from the Holistic Education Center or the respective colleges of students' majors, students can practice the skills and knowledge they learn from classes as they help marginalized groups or people from local communities, sometimes working with non-profit agencies and at other times, independently. Through learning by doing, students not only obtain professional knowledge but also develop compassion, concern, and empathy. The pedagogy has proven to create more fruitful learning experiences for both students and faculty, inspire in-depth reflection, and affirm the goodness of others in the minds of those served.

As pedagogy, service-learning also can offer a comprehensive learning experience for students. Dissolving the boundary between the ivory tower and the community, a service-learning curriculum has allowed students and faculty to sharpen their awareness about the needs of others. Through personal participation, they come to a different understanding about social justice and ethical values. Therefore, in many ways, service-learning as pedagogy has corrected the imbalance of university education in Taiwan—which used to overemphasize knowledge and skill—by implementing a platform that helps educators equalize the weight given to theory and practice (or by combining theory and real work) while simultaneously cultivating healthy emotional development.

Project Description

This section illustrates in detail a specific case of service-learning at Fu Jen by discussing the complete process for organizing a service-learning course. This case study can be a valuable reference for educators interested in designing their own service-learning curriculum. Our goal is to establish a successful model that could be applied to all schools in the country.

Curriculum development

Curriculum development at Fu Jen occurred in four stages:

- Stage One (1998): Individual teachers experimented with combining their classes with social service. It was especially popular among courses offered in the Department of Social Work and Department of Sociology.
- Stage Two (1999–2000): The unit in charge of promoting service-learning designed various patterns for service-learning and invited teachers in the Holistic Education Curriculum, especially teachers who taught philosophy of life, to take part voluntarily.
- Stage Three (2001–05): With a grant from the MOE, the university was able to implement the service-learning curriculum on a larger scale. During this stage, professors from all academic units within the university could apply for a subsidy to incorporate service-learning into their classes.
- Stage Four (2005–08): A specialized office was established to promote the service-learning program. The office coordinates resources, manages administrative work, and facilitates cooperation among all the parties involved in service-learning.

Curriculum content

The content of Fu Jen's service-learning curriculum can be broadly categorized into six major types:

- *Holistic education:* This curriculum is designed for courses under the Holistic Education Program and involved required courses for all undergraduate students at Fu Jen, including Introduction to University Life, Philosophy of Life, and Professional Ethics. Service-learning is integrated as an essential part of these courses.

- *Professional curriculum:* Designed for the professional courses in academic departments, service-learning under the professional curriculum requires students to apply their knowledge and training while providing service to the community. For example, the Social Work Department requires students to work with socially marginalized communities; the Department of Business Administration assists the construction of an aboriginal commercial zone; and the Department of Public Health helps design general plans for community health care.
- *Integrated service-learning:* In an integrated program, professors across disciplinary boundaries cooperate to address a common issue and provide an integrated scheme to a designated social group. For example, a project might focus on foreign brides, aborigines, or cultural/creative artists.
- *Community-based service-learning:* Under this category, different service-learning courses are clustered by demographics and specific community needs of the regions neighboring the university, such as Linkuo, Taishan, and Hsinchuan. In the past, services have included activities designed for senior citizens child/parent counseling, guided tours of a library and museum, and public education activities.
- *Adoption service-learning:* Through adoption service-learning, the university establishes long-term relationships with the parties being served. Prominent projects under this category include: (1) an online reading group in which the Fu Jen students serve as mentors by helping elementary students read picture books; and (2) remedial classes for children from disadvantaged families.
- *International outreach program:* The university cooperates with international organizations, such as the House of the Dying and Destitute in Calcutta, India, or the Medical and Social Services Corps in Mongolia. The faculty and students who are interested in overseas service volunteer to participate in the International Outreach Program.

Formation of participating students and faculty

The university provides preparatory courses to initiate students participating in the service-learning program with the knowledge and skills needed for volunteer work. Student leaders take part in regular workshops and long-term counseling so they can guide their fellow classmates to more successfully complete the tasks assigned and make the service experiences more rewarding. All faculty members participating in service-learning attend seminars at regular intervals so they can brainstorm curriculum design and share experiences while simultaneously learning project management skills. Core members of the service-learning program organize activities and facilitate administrative work to aid the long-term professional development of faculty and students.

Recognizing the community's needs

Reading is key to child development in that it helps to motivate learning and develop linguistic, imaginative, and creative capacities; therefore, it is critical to provide an ideal environment that encourages reading as early as possible. For years, neural scientists in Taiwan have been advocating the concept that "reading is the root of creativity" (the concept was proposed by Taiwan's former minister of education Cheng Chi-lang; see Education Bureau of Miao-Li County 2005, 32). With the rapid changes in educational, social, and technological developments over the past few years, lifestyles, work, and learning patterns have changed drastically. Computer literacy has become essential for all citizens. More than that, skills to apply information technology have become a major index for a nation's competitiveness; therefore improving computer literacy has become a common goal for many developed/developing countries. As educators facing a new wave of the revolution in learning, we have been thinking about ways to link reading and computer literacy—in other words, how to use information technology to improve the overall curriculum in reading, especially when resources are relatively scarce. To stop the widening gap between the rich and poor in Taiwan, we must address the needs of children from remote areas or disadvantaged families, and it is essential that we seek to remedy the situation from its roots—education.

Service-learning is an effective way to address the shortage of social resources by making good use of university students, which constitute an ample source of human workforce with adequate professional knowledge. Through service-learning curricula, university students are given an opportunity to mature their mentality and foster the spirit of service, but more importantly to establish the connection between their professional training and social service. Encouraging service-learning with disadvantaged and marginalized groups inspires the devotion and passion of the younger generation. To derive these benefits, service-learning has become a new trend in university education. From the perspective of knowledge acquisition or transmission, most university students are the privileged or the elite on the social spectrum and, therefore, have the advantage of access to education. Universities become locales that hoard knowledge and information. Service-learning is an effective way for universities to offer feedback and contribute to the community.

The development of Internet technology has revolutionized education and learning. From the positive side, the Internet offers a brand new platform for knowledge acquisition—a forum for sharing opinions and a way of making friends. Yet, more often than not, we also observe side-effects from the excessive use of new technologies. Internet overindulgence can actually jeopardize learning. However, for children in remote areas where transportation is inconvenient, the Internet can provide solutions to learning obstacles and serve as a portal to the world of learning.

Educators agree that the Internet's expansive outreach and its capacity to mobilize resources at minimal expense can be the means to reduce the discrepancy between the advantages offered by large cities compared to remote townships. Although they have experienced limited results, a number of Internet reading groups are at work to encourage reading and opinion sharing. One of the reasons for these unsuccessful attempts is the lack of a systematic operation and interactive strategy. Mere discussion and sharing of personal opinions on readings do not provide incentive to stimulate spontaneous participation. The infrastructure is well-established, but more should be done to bring about major breakthroughs in learning systems.

What follows is a case study examining the strategic alliance among different levels of educational institutions—elementary schools, high schools, and universities—and how it can implement a reading/learning platform on the Internet through service-learning curriculum at universities. By combining the virtual reading groups and the service-learning curricula, it is hoped that resources at universities can be made available to the remote areas in Taiwan, and ultimately bridge the gap between groups on opposite ends of the social spectrum.

Acknowledging challenges and establishing a concrete goal

Fu Jen initiated a project entitled "Developing a Knowledge-Sharing Based Study Group via an Internet Messaging Platform." The goal of this project is to establish a mechanism that will make social resources available to people in need in Taiwan, and help bridge the gap between cities and remote areas. Many challenges have been addressed in attempting to reach this goal.

The objectives of the literacy project at Fu Jen are as follows:

- Adopt primary schools in remote areas of Miao-Li County with online study groups.
- Assist at least 25 classes with the online study groups.

- Develop long-term service-learning cooperation with each primary school in remote areas.
- Increase the participation rate of university students in service-learning programs by 10%.
- Achieve a satisfaction rate of primary school teachers involved in the project of 80%.

If the above-mentioned goals can be reached, the project will be proven feasible and can be further promoted among schools in other counties in Taiwan.

Creating and communicating the concept

To effectively create an online knowledge-sharing study group in a way that it can encourage different social groups and readers to engage in long-term discussion and sharing, a more complete strategic plan was necessary. More than that, we needed a mechanism for integrating resources (such as reading materials and human resources), comprehensive standard operating procedures so that the model can be duplicated elsewhere, an online platform to mediate learning and sharing, and a conduit that encourages dialogue between participating students and teachers. Specific areas we addressed include:

- *Strategy:* The long-term goal of the project is for each university to adopt a primary school in remote areas by establishing an online study group. Through the alliance of universities and primary schools and the establishment of a service-learning module, the project will improve primary school students' reading ability and computer literacy while cultivating the spirit of social service among university students.
- *Vision:* Using Internet technology, the project has the capacity to penetrate the boundaries of real space and mend the gap of resources available to different social groups. Breaking through these barriers has been the key to the project as it mobilizes resources for disadvantaged groups.
- *Philosophy:* The basic philosophy of the project is to renovate learning via strategic alliances and new technology so that global knowledge can be accessed from a local village.
- *Infrastructure:* The infrastructure of the project comes from the concept of CORPS proposed by Seetoo (1999) in *Management of Non-Profit Organizations.* Seetoo breaks infrastructure into the component elements of client (C), operation team (O), resources (R), participants (P), and service package (S). Clients receiving service are primary

school students. Nonetheless, to increase the learning effects, the project will also try to involve their teachers and parents throughout the process. The operation team is the subject of the project, which is mainly composed of university teachers and students engaged in the activity. Also included in the operation team are administrative staff and teachers at the university and the primary schools. Resources required for the project include consumable materials, capital investment, equipment, and software. Administrative expenses are covered by the parties involved, and extra expenses for equipment or hardware will be obtained through fund-raising when necessary. Participants are primarily composed of the students who take service-learning courses, student volunteers on the university campus, and primary school teachers who provide on-site assistance and promote the project. The content of the service package includes two parts: (1) the study guides offered online; and (2) personal encounters through various activities during holidays or vacations. Personal encounters help strengthen commitment and increase interest in both clients and participants. Through face-to-face meetings, primary school teachers who observe students' learning and progress can offer first-hand feedback to the online tutors as a source of reference for future improvement. The interelation of the above-mentioned five elements is shown in Figure 8.1.

Organizing the infrastructure and integrating resources

The Fu Jen project integrates resources in four areas:

- *Human resources:* This project integrates primary school students who need a tutor with university students who have the skills and ability to guide them. However, the number of primary school students and university students are not always equal, so the work of the administrative team is to ensure that university students are matched with classes of students to guide and primary school students are matched with the appropriate tutor. Because online tutors provide guidance and advice on a general level, no extra professional training is necessary. University students from all academic majors are eligible to serve—a fact that may help in recruiting new members to join the project.
- *Books:* One of the most creative resource-economic strategies in the project is the establishment of the book swap mechanism. Students buy a certain book for one class, but later can exchange their book with another class. Via the book swap mechanism, each student spends

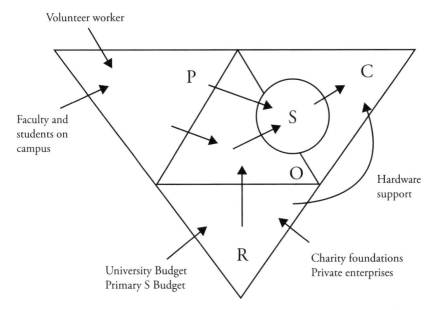

Note: Arrows signify the directions of the resource flow.

Figure 8.1 Interrelation of CORPS elements

money to buy only one book, but can access many other books. With this mechanism, students from financially disadvantaged families in remote areas do not need a huge budget for books; more importantly, circulation makes the best use of each book. The circulation also helps formulate a web of readers who read the same book and can discuss and share their opinions on the Internet.

- *Budgets:* It is important to establish a flexible and complementary budgeting process. Budgets for the Fu Jen project come from the primary schools and the university, in addition to any new funds the institutions can raise. The most expensive investment for the project is establishing the online platform and purchasing reading materials. These investments are sharable; when the online platform and the discussions enjoy a certain visibility, institutions can attract donations from charitable foundations and private enterprises.

- *Knowledge-based online study groups:* The service package is grounded in a virtual study group facilitated by an online platform. Internet technology has helped conquer what was once unconquerable—distance. With the online platform, university students can go online at home or in a dorm and guide and assist primary school students hundreds of miles away. What is more valuable in this knowledge-based online study group is that information and data can be accumulated. The study notes and discussions are open for use online, which allows others to access and read, thus adding to the value of the group.

Planning standard operating procedures

The idea for this project originates from a single class study group model (see Figure 8.2, Chart 1), which is led by a teacher. The teacher assigns a text for reading, conducts discussions, encourages idea exchanges and, if possible, further combines the reading with class materials. With advancement in information technology, using an online platform serves to multiply the effects by linking all the elements involved through the Internet: teachers, students, and reading materials. Breaking through the limitation of walls and distances among these different groups, the essential elements converge and operate on a single platform. The single-platform and multiple-class model (see Figure 8.2, Chart 2) is the model that is currently used for this project. To maximize and mobilize support and resources available throughout the country, the future of the project lies in the multiple-platform and multiple-class model (see Figure 8.2, Chart 3).

Fu Jen chose to start with the single-platform and multiple-class model because the infrastructure and operation is simpler and its success can be replicated with comparative ease.

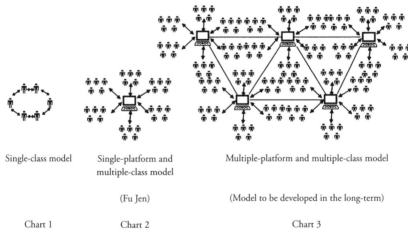

Single-class model	Single-platform and multiple-class model	Multiple-platform and multiple-class model
	(Fu Jen)	(Model to be developed in the long-term)
Chart 1	Chart 2	Chart 3

Figure 8.2 Teaching models

The standard operating procedures can be summarized as follows, and can be applied in different models:

a. Confirm the subject of the study group.
b. Understand the current situation and clients' needs.
c. Prepare the participants' qualifications and resources.
d. Conduct basic training for the participants.
e. Practice online study-group discussion and interaction.
f. Examine and reflect on the procedures and suggest improvement measures.
g. Apply the accumulated data and adjust the study guide model.
h. Encourage and facilitate dialogue between the participating teachers.
i. Expand the scale of the current program and increase the number of students profiting from the program.

This project also dissolves barriers among different teaching groups. Through regular workshops and seminars, university students and primary school teachers can meet and discuss expectations and problems of those involved in the project. The organizing administrative committee usually starts these gatherings with pre-determined issues to get things started, which can inspire teachers to conduct more in-depth dialogues. These prove to be valuable learning opportunities for both online tutors and teachers.

Executing the project

To ensure the success of our project, we executed several tasks. Based on our experience, we make the following recommendations:

- *Consult primary and university teachers to determine the content:* Because this case is a pioneering project, we use volunteers to recruit participants. Through content consultation, an interactive group is formed to get feedback. In addition, seminars and workshops are organized so that all teachers participating in the project can have a better picture and know how to contribute to the success of the project.
- *Assign tasks and establish a cooperative scheme:* Participants are assigned different tasks, such as establishing a reading list, designing the pedagogical approach, drafting evaluation methods, promoting extended activities, managing the online system, offering additional help to students, and promoting the project among peers. Throughout

the process, they are also encouraged to reflect on their individual work and give feedback to others.

- *Plan the training program (real or virtual) for participating teachers and service-learning students:* To guarantee quality education, training programs are organized on content such as computer skills, the latest developments in pedagogy for primary school students, or lessons as basic as effective communication with primary school students.

- *Organize workshops for supporting groups:* Because a large number of students and teachers are involved in this project, it is important that participants have an opportunity to share ideas and exchange experiences. When properly done, this will help recharge all the participants and improve their teaching and service, and also obtain support from the community at large.

- *Hold activities to allow real interactions:* Although the Fu Jen project's foundation is a virtual interactive platform, it still encourages parties to meet face-to-face once in a while so interactions can become more intimate. These face-to-face meetings can also make the online learning more substantial.

- *Conduct an end-of-semester showcase:* To guarantee that the project achieves its goals, we plan and host an end-of-semester showcase for all participants to present their work and the project's execution. Students can examine their own work while also learning from the work of others.

- *Inspire creativity in pedagogy and boost the quality of learning:* The large amount of materials accumulated online can be a valuable asset for researchers and inspire them to help renovate teaching and pedagogy.

- *Maintain a quality knowledge-based platform:* The platform used in this project is KMS software, designed by the primary school teachers in Miao-Li County. The server is based on the opinion exchange platform at the Miao-Li County Information Center. (Visit http://books.mlc.tw for more details.) With the ever-changing advancement in information technology, we need to make sure that we can keep updating and expanding the functions and bandwidth. Currently, managerial functions of the KMS software include the ability to upload and download files, manage Internet files, and manage accounts. The web site offers a page browser, visitor counter, discussion board, message board, and so forth. More functions are being discussed and developed.

Results

The knowledge-sharing study group is composed of primary school teachers from 19 schools in Miao-Li County. Before allying with the service-learning curriculum at Fu Jen, 79 teachers participated in the study group, and their work involved approximately 2,000 students. The group started official operation in August 2006, and by March 8 the number of participating study groups was up to 61 (each book has an individual web site). Reader counts browsing the web sites amounted to 52,352 and students generated 9,652 reading journals, 38,589 discussion articles, 6,862 creative essays, and 13,652 opinion exchanges.

To assist teachers who operate these online study groups and to invite more teachers in remote areas to join in the project, the service-learning curricula adopted the online study groups and established an alliance with Miao-Li County. The alliance officially began in April 2007. (More details are available at http://books.mlc.tw.) It was estimated that the program would grow by 50% with the participation of student tutors from Fu Jen.

Reflecting on Results

The Fu Jen project is the first of its kind in that it tries to establish a strategic alliance between primary schools and a university via the Internet. Because there are no precedents, participants must grope their way along, exploring solutions to problems and making adjustments as the project continues. By 2007, we had already discovered a list of measures to improve the project's operation, including:

- *Compile a comprehensive handbook:* As the project involves a great number of participants, we have need of a handbook to outline our standard operating procedures so successful experiences could be duplicated and pitfalls avoided.
- *Reinforce interactions between teachers and strengthen a sense of community:* Because of the limitations of physical distance, student tutors, primary school teachers, and faculty at the university cannot manage to meet as often as they would like. In addition to virtual meetings, we also encourage teachers who are not blocked by distance to meet regularly so that the cooperation can be reinforced by a sense of community and friendship, which will in turn foster the growth of and continuation of the project.
- *Establish a scheme to mobilize resources and simplify the communication process:* The project is powered by volunteers and the resources they can

invest. Because the alliance is young, it is important to facilitate strong communication, especially about the allotment of resources (i.e., to avoid missing important items or creating redundancy). If the project is successful and later expands, we will need to establish a clear set of regulations to limit miscommunications.

• *Establish a blueprint for the future:* The current project is a pioneering experiment to create a blueprint for a more comprehensive program. If a clear vision is not available at an earlier stage, it becomes difficult for participants to build on and invest in the project. Therefore, we think it is essential that a comprehensive (e.g., national) blueprint should be created at the conclusion of this experiment.

Goals for Future Development

The project has successfully helped build an alliance between primary schools and a university. By April 2007, the operation of the alliance was running smoothly. We anticipate a promising future. Our plans include:

• *Inviting more primary schools to participate in the project so more students can benefit:* When we can duplicate the single-platform/multiple-class pattern with a multiple-platform/multiple-class module, more students throughout the country can join the online study group and enjoy free tutoring from university students.

• *Motivating more universities to participate in service-learning curricula:* Compared to traditional one-on-one tutoring, the online study guide is much more economic and is not limited by time and space. Therefore, if more universities are willing to participate in the project, we can effectively and comprehensively improve the reading ability and computer literacy of primary school students. The tentative goal is for each university to adopt one county.

• *Exploring Internet resources and inspiring creative teaching:* The execution of this online knowledge-sharing based study group project allows the accumulation of knowledge. It offers an open resource for teachers who seek inspiration for teaching and researchers who conduct studies on pedagogy. These will all instill new life and vitality into the teaching and learning web in Taiwan.

• *Stimulating the formation of online study groups between social groups:* Many associations and groups are promoting the concept of online learning and sharing, yet the result is not quite satisfactory. The concept and practice of this project can stimulate the work of these different alliances so that a national web of reading can be made possible.

- *Establish a Chinese knowledge-sharing study group worldwide:* One of the charms of an online platform is that it transcends physical boundaries. When readers can get online, they can be a member of any study group they choose. With the advancement in information technology, Taiwan has the potential to be the hub of online Chinese study groups when the software and reading materials have been abundantly accumulated. We look forward to a future when Taiwan can provide a portal to the world of Chinese-related knowledge and broadcast it to the world.

Service-learning is conducive to the formation of students' personalities. It helps to perfect their professional knowledge and leadership competence, and thus can contribute significantly to the fulfillment of a university's educational goals. While confirming the positive effects of service-learning programs in university education, we have also discovered certain weak links that must be further strengthened and challenges that must be conquered:

- A more solid theoretical grounding should be established so that the validity and acceptance of the pedagogy can be established in linking service and learning.
- To assure students' professional competence, activities of service-learning should be tailored to meet the teaching goals and purposes of each service-learning course they take.
- Designs in service-learning activities should be further examined to advance the quality of service provided.
- The university and non-profit agencies should develop more solid and long-term relationships so experiences can be accumulated and positive effects continued.
- More can be done to create and explore new patterns of service-learning using the Internet and online technology.
- More can be done to promote the comprehensive understanding of the concept of service-learning in communities in general and to coordinate the resources available.

Conclusion

This detailed illustration of the service-learning class epitomizes the philosophy of Fu Jen Catholic University in the promotion of its service-learning curriculum and how it relates to the university's more general educational goals. It is a successful example of a service-learning program in that it correctly identifies the need of a marginalized social group, coordinates resources available, engages the service providers and receivers in a productive and rewarding way, and allows communication across different social groups. It is a perfect way for a university, which used to be regarded as an ivory tower, to respond to the need of the community through positive actions.

With the advent of "knowledge economy" in the twenty-first century, human talents become our most valuable asset. Service-learning, as pedagogy for higher education, has proven to be one of the most effective ways to cultivate talented executives and administrators with a sense of compassion and empathy. Thus, an increasing number of universities have incorporated service-learning into their academic curricula, which has transformed the traditional modules of teaching and learning on university campus. As a pioneer in the promotion of service-learning, Fu Jen has spared no effort to share experiences with her counterparts in Taiwan and other countries, while absorbing the successful undertakings of others so more can be done to perfect the service-learning program—an endeavor which bears infinite potential to change our world for the better.

9 | International Service-learning: A Singapore Experience

Dennis Lee

There is a need to look again at what we are educating for and to create learning environments which are attentive to students' and teachers' attitudes and which maximize the potential for learning despite individual differences . . . A major component of such learning environments must be opportunities for not only abstract but also experiential learning; that is, learning in which the learner is directly in touch with the realities being studied rather than simply reading about, hearing about, or talking about these realities.

— Joint statement of the Association for Experiential Education,
the Council for Adult and Experiential Learning, and the
National Society of Internships and Experiential Education (Kendall, 1990, 3)

If we were to examine with candor how well traditional study abroad programs fulfill our stated idealistic goals for developing international/intercultural knowledge and understanding, would we find congruence between rhetoric and reality? Or would we admit that, in many cases at least, the program represents a transplanted home campus environment, classroom-based, lecture-oriented, Euro-centered, with little direct and intentional use of the experience of the other country or culture as the curriculum?

— Howard A. Berry (1985, 24)

Singapore education has emphasized the importance of promoting experiential education, community service, and enrichment activities such as research and a career-related work stint. While great effort has been made to engage youths in community service, it places little emphasis on learning from the experiences gained. On the other hand, as a part of experiential education, service-learning endeavors to combine both service and knowledge, placing an emphasis on learning commensurate with service. According to Howard Berry

(1988, 3), service-learning is "the union of public and Community Service with structured Intentional Learning."

Service-learning differs from community service in three ways. First, service-learning programs explicitly foster participants' learning about the larger social issues behind the human needs to which they are responding. This includes understanding the historical, sociological, cultural, and political contexts of the need or issue being addressed. Service-learning programs may have several types of learning goals in this reflective component—intellectual, civil, ethical, moral, cross-cultural, career, and personal. However, the needs of the host community, rather than of the learning goals, come first in defining the service, and the community defines those needs. An international service-learning experience might help youth see issues from a global perspective. This is helpful for developing the skills and awareness needed for responsible global citizenship. Thus, the "community" in the definition of international service-learning programs can refer to the local neighbourhood as well as state, national, or international communities. International service-learning programs build structures (e.g., pre-service preparation, seminars, group discussions, journals, readings, debriefs) that actively support participants to learn from their service experiences.

The second factor that distinguishes service-learning from community service is an emphasis on reciprocity. Reciprocity is the exchange of giving and receiving between the "server" and the person or group being served. Service-learning avoids the traditionally paternalistic, one-way approach to service in which one person or group has the resources, which they share charitably or voluntarily with the person or group that lacks resources. In service-learning, those being served control the service provided. The needs of the community determine what the service tasks will be. It is this reciprocity that creates a sense of mutual responsibility and respect between individuals in the service-learning exchange, which avoids the ever-present pitfall of paternalism disguised under the name of service. Do those served grow as persons; do they become healthier, wiser, freer, and more autonomous, or further deprived? The aim of the participants' service should be the collaborative development and empowerment of those served. It is this form of exchange that fosters a sense of responsibility between participants and is a building block for them to show esteem for one another.

Third, in service-learning, all are learners and have significant control over what is learned. The learning needs of the participants must be negotiated and well matched with the needs of the host organization. The critical task is making sure that services rendered are not overwhelmed by the learning tasks. Often, unplanned learning will occur that will challenge value assumptions and require thoughtful reflection and sharing with others. This third factor emphasizes that every participant in a service-learning program is a learner, and determines what is to be learned. Nevertheless, there must be a balance between the service provided and the learning objectives. It is vital to ensure that the emphasis on both is equal.

An important aspect of international service-learning is its ability to enhance international and intercultural literacy, knowledge, and sensitivity. This aspect is mandatory because it is a building block that brings service and learning into a synergy regardless of the physical location (Berry 1988). It teaches participants to grow and learn based on constant advice and constructive criticism from their peers and mentors.

This chapter reflects on an international service-learning program based on the experiential learning framework of David Kolb (1984). Kolb's theory describes learning as successive stages of concrete experience, reflective observation, abstract conceptualization, and active experimentation. This is a foundation for the pedagogical process of service-learning. The program discussed within this framework was initiated by the Singapore International Foundation. From 2000 to 2005, the Youth Expedition Project sent more than 12,000 youths across the Association of Southeast Nations, China, and India to execute international service-learning projects. Each group averaged 20 youths and was led by expedition leaders and facilitators. Subsequently, the National Junior College embarked on its unique student-led, parent-mentored international service-learning projects beginning in 2005 and continuing through 2006. The experiences gathered from several thousands of participants on international service-learning trips will be used to reflect on the applicability of the best practices suggested by Honnet and Poulsen (1996).

Methodology

This chapter is structured as an academic interaction with several papers extracted from the work of Jane C. Kendall and Associates (1990). Reflections and experiences have been brought to bear using this interaction. I have conducted a sample survey of international service-learning project participants (17-year-olds) implemented by National Junior College in Singapore, and reviewed the responses of these participants to find out how they have grown through their international service-learning experiences. The tool used is an international service-learning questionnaire, which had the main goal of gathering honest feedback about the program with a specific focus on personal and leadership development.[1] The survey was administered to ascertain areas of success, areas for improvement, and the level of character and leadership development that the international service-learning experience has given to its participants.

Principles of an Effective International Service-learning Program

In the implementation of international service-learning projects, the Singapore International Foundation attempted to apply ten best practices suggested by Honnet and Poulsen (1996), as discussed in this section.

Engage people in responsible and challenging actions for the common good

A prerequisite for an effective international service-learning program project is that it must serve the needs of the community and the common good. It must be something the host partners regard as important, and a need as defined by the community. Our volunteers actively engage in this exercise with our partners. For example, we attempt to apply this principle in projects such as primary health education programs, refurbishment of school classrooms, and rural computer literacy training programs. A participant reflects on an experience:

> Participants of the international service-learning program encountered several challenges. During the pre-activity discussions and on-site learning phases of the program, numerous challenging decisions had to be made. Some of us participants were assigned to deal with administrative matters and were required to find best-value air tickets, do research on and recommend the appropriate health vaccinations to all the participants, and request free excess baggage on flights to transport project materials, such as blankets and books to Myanmar. Those of us responsible for logistics had to learn to network with corporate sponsors and negotiate win-win situations, presenting benefits to the sponsors. For instance, we had to take into consideration what kind of computer specifications sponsors would be willing to provide for the Tam Thon Hiep Open House in Vietnam.

As observed by Hedin and Conrad (1980), proponents of action- and service-learning claim that by placing youths in responsible roles in which their actions affect others, more responsible attitudes and behaviours will develop.

Provide structured opportunities for people to reflect critically on their service experience

Through a facilitation process and deliberate program design that harnesses the principles of adventure education, expeditionary learning, and other cogent pedagogies, volunteers constantly reflect on their experiences and what they have learned. The reflection process is intentional and continuous throughout their experience.

Through daily observations, discussions, journaling exercises, and similar activities, and through exposure to real problems, including moral, ethical, and civic issues confronting the host and home country, volunteers understand more about personal responsibility, principles of good governance, and civic responsibility. Many of the discussions include feedback from host partners and the communities concerned. Another participant observes:

> Our international service-learning program places a great emphasis on critical reflections. Nightly group reflection sessions were held. This is where intense critical discussions and sharing of ideas left our participants with a deeper understanding of the relevant issues. Feedback was gathered not just from other fellow participants, but also from our parent mentors involved in the program. We also conducted individual reflections in the form of writing, especially keeping a journal.
>
> By analyzing and solving our problems, we were able to look at our experiences with hindsight and conduct the necessary and effective actions afterward. Such opportunity for feedback and reflection helped our participants to grow intellectually.

This participant's reflection shows how experience and education intertwine, and how experience serves both as the source of knowledge and a process of knowing—education is of, by, and for experience (Hedin and Conrad 1980).

Articulate clear service and learning goals for everyone involved

Throughout all phases of the expeditions and especially at the pre-expedition stage, the volunteers and service recipients decide what is to be accomplished and what is to be learned. These service and learning goals are agreed upon after in-depth discussions with all the parties, and in the context of the traditions and cultures of the host community. The concept of reciprocity is expressly highlighted and explained to host partner communities, organizations, leaders, facilitators, and volunteers. Each expedition team is assigned a mentor-facilitator who will guide all parties to understand and apply this fundamental principle in international service-learning. The application of this principle is described by a participant:

Our program certainly carved out clear service and learning goals. All of us, as service providers, had a good understanding of the learning objectives of the program. Our objectives were to understand different cultures, see issues from a global perspective, and acquire competencies such as organizing and planning. Participants that went to Vietnam were clear on the goals: to source for used computers, install an English Language Program into these computers to facilitate teaching English, and renovate a playground for a school. Participants who went to Myanmar aimed to set up a library to provide English books and build latrines and tube wells for villagers.

Allow for those with needs to define those needs

Project needs are defined by the recipients of the service in addition to the community groups and constituencies to which they belong. Defining needs is a process of negotiation and in-depth discussions to arrive at a mutual understanding that results in suitable projects to address the needs of the community. One such project involved setting up a computer lab in Kompong Cham province, two hours away from Phnom Penh, the capital of Cambodia. After six months of fact-finding and discussion with many parties (including groups of economically disadvantaged students) the volunteers concluded that such a need was real, and that the effort would be a sustained one from the organizers of the expedition and the youth association receiving the service. The computer lab is now bustling with classes and serves the needs of economically disadvantaged students.

An effective service-learning program should provide service according to the needs of the people they are helping. Yet, this is only possible if those being served are clearly aware of and understand their needs. As reflected in this participant's experience, if they are not clear on their needs, help must be provided to assist them in defining their needs:

The international service-learning project leader communicated with those being served to get a rough idea of how they could be helped, while the YMCA organization helped to clarify and define the needs. With the YMCA helping both service providers and service recipients to come to an understanding, the service recipients' needs could be understood, and we could have a good idea of how to help them. However, we had to first ensure that we were not taking jobs from the local community. We had to help the service recipients in areas that would otherwise go undone, and not in areas that members of their local community could finish without external help.

Clarify the responsibilities of each person and organization involved

The mentor-facilitator guides the development of the project. The host partner and the organizer would have decided on the allocation and assignment of roles and responsibilities at the pre-expedition stage. Feedback is gathered and discussions held throughout the expedition process to clarify roles, responsibilities and learning objectives for the project. A participant explains:

> The students were assigned to three teams: Administrative, Learning, and Logistics. Each group played a different role in the overall organization of the project. Their roles were clearly defined and did not overlap (i.e., all the group tasks were differentiated).
>
> Also, parents on the trip played their part as parent mentors in guiding us according to corporate standards and exposing us to the ways of the globalized world. While most of us are used to being judged according to academic standards, this is not enough. The parent mentors emphasized that the students were to complete their assigned tasks well and not just at a satisfactory level.
>
> All members of the trip, students and parents alike, also aimed to improve family ties by working together in the organizing and laboring portions of the trip. This helped foster character development and was beneficial to the students.

Match service providers and service needs through a process that recognizes changing circumstances

National Junior College international service-learning projects and the Youth Expedition Project are cross-cultural, and changes occur frequently due to miscommunication and different expectations. Developing a process that ensures continuous feedback about the changing circumstances and people-to-people dynamics is important. Leaders were trained to deal with the changing circumstances that might affect the group. Learning objectives among individuals changed and adaptation was required. A participant reflects on how one project adapted:

> Services provided on the trip were affected by the changing service needs of the service recipients. We had to be flexible and adapt to the changing circumstances. Also, we constantly reflected on what was already accomplished, and gave feedback so that we could further improve on what had not yet been done.
>
> When teaching phonics to Vietnamese locals, one of our teams first started out by using the English language software we had brought over from Singapore. However, we soon found that the locals had very little knowledge of using computers and had difficulty understanding what was taught. The team decided to

revise their plan, to teach the locals phonics and the English alphabet instead. This received a good response and many of the locals learned and understood quickly.

On the second day of the trip to Vietnam, a typhoon hit the area and we were unable to travel to the work site. This meant that one day of work was gone, and we would have to complete two days worth of work the next day. By reflecting on this event and adapting to the situation, more manpower was allocated to jobs that were more intensive. Emphasis was placed on speed and efficiency, to ensure that the restoration could be completed in time.

Expect genuine, active and sustained organizational commitment

A participant discusses an international service-learning project in Myanmar that was developed with a three-year time-frame to provide tube wells and latrines for the fire victims of Hlaing Thayar township who were relocated to a new ward at Swi Pytha township:

> Continual commitment was observed from both the service providers and the service recipients in our international service-learning program. The volunteers and authorities at the YMCA were enthusiastic about us providing service to their country and helped us facilitate the running of the program. Many of us also showed an ongoing commitment, showing conscientious planning and dedication to the program. Out of the students who participated in the 2005 international service-learning trip to Myanmar, many of them continued their participation in the subsequent year.

Use training, supervision, monitoring, support, recognition, and evaluation to meet service and learning goals

Significant importance is placed on training, supervision, and monitoring progress throughout the implementation of each expedition. The leaders and participants receive substantial training before they leave for the expedition. This includes training programs, cultural orientation, language, and other related training. Evaluation occurs both at the expedition level and the host-country level, together with our partners. A participant explains:

> Supervision, monitoring, and support were shown in this project. Student leaders ensured that the committee completed the tasks delegated, while parent mentors attached to individual committees supervised the progress of work. Recognition and credit was given to participants of this program, and each participant received a certificate of participation. Evaluation to meet service and learning goals was done every day during the trip. Post-expedition evaluation was also conducted. This evaluation will be used to improve on the program for the following year.

Ensure that the time commitment for service is flexible, appropriate, and in the best interests of all involved

The scope of the service must be feasible and practical. Some projects that require a longer duration to complete were executed in phases by the organizers over a three-year period. A participant observed:

> The international service-learning program involves three phases: Pre-activity discussions, on-site service-learning and post-expedition debriefing. During the planning stage, sufficient time was allocated for preliminary preparation, cultural research, and setting the groundwork. The amount of time allocated was agreed by all parties.
>
> A great amount of commitment was seen during the planning and execution phases. However, commitment from the participants was not as rigorous during the post-trip phase. This program is sustainable, because it has been running for two years. A majority of us also expressed interest in participating in this program again.

Commit to program participation by and with diverse populations

While the National Junior College international service-learning project targeted Singaporean youths, an integral component of the expedition is to include persons from different ethnic, racial, cultural, and religious backgrounds. This is achieved through the inclusion of international students studying at National Junior College and youths from overseas partner communities throughout the project. The program did not discriminate against any particular group; it consisted of people from different ethnic, racial and religious backgrounds, and a good mix of genders.

Rewards of Reflections

An intrinsic aspect of the intentional learning practice requires participants to apply David Kolb's reflective observation method through journaling and group discussions. As participants of service-learning projects embark on this exercise, several benefits can be derived (Conrad and Hedin 1987).[2]

Academic learning

Improved reading, writing and speaking abilities: Writing about and discussing experiences and reading about their area of service is an engaging way for participants to practice these basic skills, as observed by this youth:

Daily reflection helped us to consolidate our learning experiences and share with one another on the striking events of the day. The sharing helped us to be concise in phrasing our different learning experiences and the importance of substantiating and explaining our various viewpoints. The reflection helped us to voice our opinions with clarity and share our feelings. We learned more about universal issues such as poverty and humanitarian aid.

Better learning of subject matter: Participants learn not only about one particular subject, but also about the interrelationship between that subject and other (societal) issues. A learner shares what this means:

Through reflections, we were able to explain and describe our learning experiences and developed these into abstract conceptualization. For example, the people there were poverty-stricken, but were contented with life. These observations prompted thought-provoking questions such as: 'Does monetary wealth bring human beings true happiness and contentment? Is it better to be rich but miserable, or poor but happy?' We each learned a valuable lesson on the principles of life. Such questions also led us to discuss . . . the history of each country and the importance of having good governance.

Learning to learn from experience: Reflection is a cluster of skills, involving observation, asking questions, and putting facts, ideas, and experiences together to add new meaning to them all. A youth expressed it this way:

Reflections led us to think of areas of improvement as a result of our experience. We were made aware of the essential social and service skills needed for us to improve over the subsequent days. The combined effect of reflection tied every aspect of the international service-learning experience together. It helped us to see a broader picture and ultimately realize our roles in a larger community context, developing us into better leaders through experience.

Personal development

Awareness of changes in oneself: On-going reflection helps to reveal what personal changes are occurring in self-image, skills, ideas about people, and thoughts about a career. Articulating them to others make those changes stick. One youth reflected on the advantages of reflection:

With active reflection, we managed to pull out our strengths and weaknesses and developed different aspects of ourselves. These include personal, leadership, and service characteristics. We constantly looked back at our lives and considered what could be done to bring about greater personal growth and development. Some of us also noted a slight change in our attitudes towards service. We described our acclimatization and assimilation into both the physical and cultural aspects of the Lijiang, China.

A sense of community: Meeting with other volunteers provides the opportunity to share successes and failures, to call on others for help and advice, and to gain support, recognition, and a sense of belonging to some greater effort. A youth observed:

> The entire trip helped us to generate a greater sense of [community] service. We saw ourselves as fortunate and felt the need to contribute to a slightly less privileged society in our own capacity and capability. We bonded together as fellow volunteers and as peers and even built an international service-learning community among ourselves. The reflection that we went through fostered this common understanding and camaraderie between us, helping us to see the benefits of our service to the communities. Reflections made us more aware of how a little something goes a long way if the intention is sincere and genuine from the start.

Taking charge of life: Being able to learn from experience gives participants the power to influence the meaning and impact of things they do or that happen to them. It also puts them in charge. The process is revealed by this youth:

> From reflection sessions, we were prompted to consider where we were heading in life, our future plans and possible careers. We reflected on our goals in life, and how we wanted our lives to be. The parent mentors not only encouraged us to reflect more on these, but also gave insights on the corporate world and how certain issues could be perceived from a global perspective, thus exposing us to ways of the working world.

Program improvement

Improved service: Reflection improves the quality of service. The more practical the sessions, the more energetically the volunteers will participate, as shared by this participant:

> We are able to notice that the international service-learning (Myanmar) 2006 team had improvement in service compared to the international service-learning (Myanmar) 2005 team. The post-debrief sharing sessions of the 2005 team enabled us to be more prepared in 2006. Daily reflections and sharing of experiences allowed us to look at areas which we could improve on.

Improved program: For a project leader, feedback from participants on how things were going and discussions of how to make them better was invaluable. One project leader reflected:

> Feedback brought up certain issues, such as having greater student involvement in active leadership roles to foster character and leadership development. This was not well-achieved in the international service-learning 2005 program as we did not play an active enough role in the planning of the trip. From then on, the importance of leadership was stressed to all of us, the committee heads making sure that each of us had a specific leadership role. We learned to see how our individual contribution would add to the overall success of the international service-learning program.

Character Development from International Service-learning

For the purposes of the National Junior College's "ISL-Leadership and Character Development" Survey, character development consists of five virtues: loyalty, perseverance, patience, servitude, and empathy. It is crucial for us to have a sense of loyalty, because we should have a sense of pride in our identity and where we come from. Perseverance, as another virtue, holds the key to a more fulfilling life because it helps us to overcome the trials and tribulations we face. With it, we are able to see the greater goal that lies at the end of the road. Patience is an important virtue for us to develop because we should plan one step at a time to reach the end goal. Servitude and empathy form the basis of a good servant leader who has other interests before his or her own, and focuses on helping people in need.

As illustrated in Figure 9.1, almost all the respondents to the questionnaire strongly agreed or agreed that they had developed in terms of these virtues, and nearly all respondents felt they had been given specific leadership roles in one form or another. The anomalies were a result of the participant's inability to commit their time to the planning phase of the project due to other co-curricular and academic commitments. All respondents replied that they believe they have developed in character and leadership qualities through the international service-learning program.

Included here are two responses to the question, "In what ways do you feel that you have developed your leadership and character through the international service-learning experience?"

> I have learned to treasure what I have even more than before. The international service-learning experience has also molded my character by motivating me to be

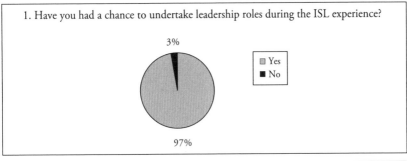

1. Have you had a chance to undertake leadership roles during the ISL experience?

3%

☐ Yes
■ No

97%

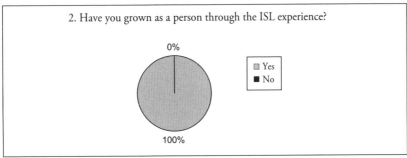

2. Have you grown as a person through the ISL experience?

0%

☐ Yes
■ No

100%

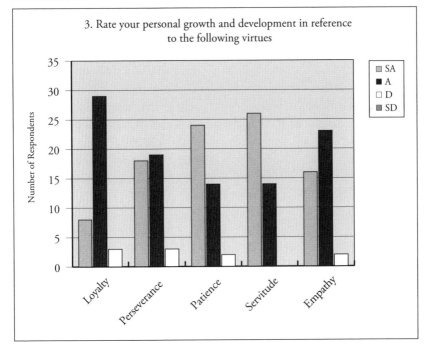

3. Rate your personal growth and development in reference to the following virtues

☐ SA
■ A
☐ D
■ SD

NB: SA stands for "Strongly Agree," A stands for "Agree," D stands for "Disagree," and SD stands for "Strongly Disagree."

Figure 9.1   Survey results of National Junior College integrated program students

more determined and to learn to be more independent. In terms of leadership, I have come to understand and appreciate the distinct leadership styles of others and work with them effectively.

— Tan Xin Pei, co-head of the logistics committee

I have learned how to be tolerant even at times when everything is not going right, the frequent reflection sessions help me to learn the importance of reflection and I have emerged as a more reflective person, constantly checking on myself. I was also able to lead in a non-major role. I developed my perseverance and was able to push through the hard times, when we were asked to do things beyond our ability. I learnt that the joy of serving people is really a driving force for wanting to serve and I learnt of more ways that I can serve the community. Everyone is a leader in their little ways.

— Soh Rong'en, co-head of the administrative committee

Leadership Development from International Service-learning

To what extent is an effective international service-learning program relevant to leadership development? According to Stanton (1988), there is a strong connection. He stresses the need for the pedagogy of service-learning in leadership education and public service in higher education. He suggests that service-learning involves more than applying leadership abilities, but is "more importantly, a catalyst for their development" (1988, 338).

The international service-learning program has allowed participants to develop a few aspects of their leadership abilities. An effective leader needs to have a sense of vision and accountability for his/her actions. International service-learning participants have learned that a clear goal is essential in order to complete a task, and as leaders, they set out to have their fellow participants cooperate with them in order to meet the goal.

Responsibilities were placed on the leader to ensure that all operations went smoothly and according to schedule. Though it cannot be said that the international service-learning participants could learn enough about the context in which they were working, they could exercise good discernment and perception based on the circumstances they were facing. They learned the importance of fostering good interpersonal relationships and effective communication. Situational leadership was practiced.

An international service-learning program is therefore highly relevant to leadership development. As Stanton (1988) observes, "[t]he pedagogy of service-learning, by linking responsible participation in our 'untidy world' with a complete cycle of self-reflective learning, provides an essential bridge for linking personal empowerment (and community empowerment!) with cognitive growth" (Stanton 1988, 338).

Conclusion

Using Kolb's experiential learning framework, international service-learning experiences have yielded good results in developing participants in character and leadership. International service-learning bridges a gap between theory and reality, and has extended learning beyond the traditional classroom.

> If you give people fish, they can eat for a day.
> If you teach them how to fish they can eat for a lifetime.
> If you teach them to learn, they don't have to eat fish all their life.
>
> —Tom Smith[3]

10 | A Cross-cultural Service-learning Program Model: W.T. Chan Fellowships Program

Jane Szutu Permaul

Seldom do we have an opportunity to design a cross-cultural service-learning program grounded in the best theories available. The W. T. Chan Fellowships Program, sponsored by the Lingnan Foundation, however, offered such an opportunity. The program was designed to honor Professor W. T. Chan, academic dean (1930–36) of the former Lingnan University in Guangzhou, China, and professor of Chinese culture at Dartmouth College in Hanover, New Hampshire. It was intended to reflect his values of promoting self-fulfillment and international understanding in addition to the Lingnan University motto, "Education for Service." Professor Chan received his education in China and the United States and successfully navigated both cultures as a student, teacher, and administrator in higher education. Consequently, the design of the Chan fellowships program involves two major characteristics for the participants: a cross-cultural experience and a service-learning experience, with the goal of providing opportunities for self-fulfillment through international exposure and social/community service. The Chan fellowships program, which began in 2000, has evolved into a cross-cultural service-learning program, with the potential to become a model for other programs with similar goals.

This chapter describes the program design, which is based on the application of existing theories, and shares the findings of cross-cultural learning outcomes acquired by fellows. It introduces a documentation tool that may prove to be helpful in furthering research and assessing experience-based learning programs. It describes the essential elements in designing a cross-cultural service-learning program and tests a methodology for documenting learning outcomes that informs their effectiveness.

Program Design

Although community, social, and volunteer services have long been a part of Asian-Pacific cultures, the notion of service-learning as a pedagogic strategy or part of a curriculum in post-secondary education is relatively new. Service-learning refers to a form of learning in which learners render service to others, usually through one or more agencies in the local community. The learner is sponsored and supervised by an educational institution working in partnership with host agencies. The learning objectives and outcomes vary depending on the particular service-learning program's goals. These learning objectives and outcomes can be subject/discipline-based (e.g., chemistry related to air pollution, economics related to availability of natural resources, literature related to culture and subcultures, gerontology related to public policies for the elderly) or they can be cognitive and affective learning (e.g., interpersonal relationships, communication, problem-solving, leadership, adaptability, flexibility). The learning objectives are usually determined jointly by learners and the educational institution offering the opportunity.

Programs involving young people visiting and working in another country are far from a new phenomenon. Most programs assume that cross-cultural learning and sensitivity occurs as international visitors interact with a culture different from their own. Cross-cultural learning and sensitivity refers to a conscious awareness of similarities and differences in two or more cultures by the people involved. When that knowledge and sensitivity are lacking, a particular behavior can convey different meaning when filtered through different cultural norms. For example, a host family in the United States may treat a Chan fellow as a family member, expecting the fellow to behave like other family members instead of a guest, as a genuine expression of welcome and inclusion into the daily life of the family. However, the fellows' cultural conditioning may lead them to think the host is being aloof and inattentive by leaving them to do whatever they want. Similarly, in a workplace in the United States, minimal supervision and direction may be observed with the intent of allowing the Chan fellow to pursue their interest and strengths, but the fellow may feel neglected when they do not receive specific instruction and direction. Cross-cultural learning outcomes require both cognitive and experiential learning in such situations, which involves knowing what a particular culture expects and how the expectation manifests itself behaviorally.

The W.T. Chan Fellowships Program selects 8 fellows each year and will soon expand to 12 fellows, all from Sun Yat Sen University (SYSU; also known as Zhongshan University) in Guangzhou and the Lingnan University in Hong Kong (LUHK). Fellows are selected from among upper division students (third and fourth-year undergraduates), those who have recently earned their bachelor's degree, and graduate students. Both universities assist with the recruitment, and a panel assembled by the Institute of International Education (IIE) interviews finalists individually after an application review.

The University of California at Berkeley and Los Angeles (UCB and UCLA, respectively) are the host institutions in the United States, with 4 (soon to be) Chan fellows assigned to each campus. The program design differs slightly at the two campuses. Both universities place each fellow at a non-profit agency, according to their interests and academic studies, and at an American home. Locations of the non-profit agency and the home where the fellow is staying must be within reach by public transportation, enabling the fellow to commute independently. Each campus conducts a weekly seminar; UCB emphasizes social justice and social activism and UCLA emphasizes social justice, public policies, and service ethics. The weekly seminar also extends to reflection by the fellows, linking and integrating seminar topics with their previous knowledge and their American experience. Finally, fellows are asked to write a weekly reflection paper that discusses what they have learned and issues they have experienced, and a final paper that translates their cross-cultural learning back to their home base.

The Chan fellows program is $5\frac{1}{2}$ months in length, with most fellows spending another 10 to 14 days traveling in the United States prior to returning to China. A pre-departure orientation, conducted at SYSU, is required of all fellows for the purpose of preparing them for a successful cross-cultural service-learning experience. The orientation emphasizes logistics more than skills that may prove helpful in engaging in cross-cultural service-learning. Former fellows have participated in these orientations to give incoming fellows a more personal perspective on the challenges and rewards of a cross-cultural service-learning experience. Staff from UCB, UCLA, and IIE participate to formally introduce the program and outline intended learning outcomes in addition to practical knowledge about cross-cultural issues, especially as they relate to social and community service.

Upon the fellows' arrival at Berkeley or Los Angeles, each campus conducts a more extensive 3 to 5-day orientation. This orientation helps Chan fellows with details such as establishing bank accounts, obtaining credit/debit cards and telephone cards, helping them to learn the public transit system, and giving them overall exposure to the community in which they will live and serve for more than five months. In addition, they are introduced to campus staff, their prospective host families, and the host agencies, allowing time for everyone to get acquainted. The fellows get to know each other so they can depend on each other for support during their stay away from home. During each campus orientation, the fellows live together on campus.

After the on-site orientation, fellows are placed with host families, preferably close to their host agency. Each week, they work as interns at their respective host agencies for four days and visit the host campus for one day to take part in a scheduled seminar and other campus activities. The seminar serves several purposes. One purpose is to learn cognitively about social justice and its meaning and practice in American communities, and another is to relate cognitive learning to the fellows' experiences in their respective host agencies, thus attempting to integrate cognitive and affective learning. Fellows are required to complete a weekly mini-paper highlighting what they have learned and what they are concerned about. The seminar meetings are opportunities for fellows to share their newly acquired knowledge with peers and discuss their concerns. Through this reflection and sharing process, the fellows' learning expands beyond their individual experiences. Their concerns transform into understanding through discussions with fellows and faculty. Weekends are spent with host families, attending special campus events (e.g., a football game or concert), taking part in special social agency events (e.g., organizing a clean-up event at a community school with other agency volunteers), or with other fellows for cultural-social events of their own choice (e.g., shopping, visiting a museum, traveling to visit friends and family in the United States).

As part of the seminar requirements, each fellow develops a proposal for a community service project to be implemented back home. Needs and viability for the proposed project must be well documented. At the culmination event, fellows individually present their respective proposed project to the university staff, their host families, internship host agencies, and invited guests. This is an opportunity for the American hosts to learn about Chinese culture as it relates to social and community service. It is also the time to celebrate cross-cultural learning by everyone involved and to thank the hosts for their contribution and support.

Theoretical foundation of the program design

The W.T. Chan Fellowships Program incorporates all the critical elements of learning from experience as suggested by the experiential learning theory developed by David Kolb (1984). Additionally, the program is a cross-cultural service-learning program, as evidenced by the four types of experiences fellows engage in while living in the United States. Each Chan fellow:

1. Serves as an intern in a non-profit organization and provides services to a defined community. Fellows typically spend at least 4 days each week, 8 hours each day, for 20 weeks in this environment (620 hours).

2. Lives with an American family, which can involve living with a one-person family, a single-parent family, or a more traditional two-parent family with one or more children. Fellows have their own room and eat with the host family when possible (although typical American families seldom eat meals together except for special occasions).
3. Attends a seminar on campus and participates in campus and community activities.
4. Commutes by public transit to and from home to the internship site or to campus.

All experiences are intended to enhance cross-cultural learning, while the internship and the seminar enhance learning about social justice, service to others, and instituting social change. Figure 10.1 depicts the key elements of the program design and their relationships to Kolb's experiential learning cycle.

These experiences enable fellows to continuously complete the experiential learning cycle, with learning outcomes evident by the end of the fellows' stay in the United States. Through the internship and the performance evaluations of their supervisors, fellows gain competence in technical skills such as organizing an event, assessing service needs, and directly serving clients. Beyond that, based on their seminar discussions and mini-papers, they gain a level of understanding

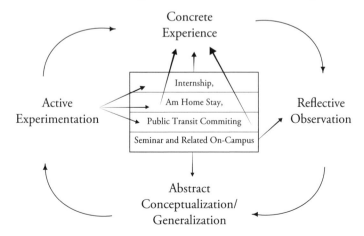

Figure 10.1 Integration of Kolb's experiential learning cycle in the design of the Chan Fellows Program

of the role of non-profit organizations and government agencies in providing needed services to targeted communities, especially the underserved. Primarily as a result of their agency experience and sharing among fellows, many learn how public and social policies can affect the availability and quality of social and community services. These technical learning outcomes are most evident from the projects they produce at the end of their fellowship.

To bolster the cross-cultural aspect of the program, fellows are intentionally placed in the most ethnically and culturally diverse American communities, where different cultures exist side by side and are integrated to some extent. The Bay Area and Los Angeles in California are two places where Chinese and Chinese-American cultures are prevalent. Based on the locations, the program assumes that the host university campuses, internship agencies, and homes all have some familiarity with Chinese-American culture and are knowledgeable enough to experientially introduce American culture to the visiting fellows. The program requires all fellows to possess functional verbal and written English skills. It assumes that the fellows have enough familiarity with American culture to give them confidence to venture out on their own. These program characteristics are based on studies on the successful learning outcomes of language immersion programs (Cohen et al. 2005, Genesee 1987).

Specific cross-cultural learning outcomes have been difficult to document. With seven cohorts having successfully completed the program, questions regarding its cross-cultural aspects remain:

- Does the Kolb experiential learning theory apply to cross-cultural learning?
- If so, what sort of cross-cultural learning occurs? What might be the learning outcomes?
- Is the W. T. Chan fellowship program design adequate to allow participants to develop cross-cultural skills and understanding?
- Is cross-cultural learning a one-way or two-way learning experience? Do the American hosts learn anything along with the fellows?
- Can the design be strengthened to generate deeper understanding and integration of different cultures?

These questions prompted further study on the cross-cultural aspect of service-learning and experiential program design.

Literature Review

Cross-cultural learning has been studied from different perspectives, all of which informs this study. Ramburuth (2001) discovered that, because of cultural differences, students from Asian countries approach studying and learning differently compared to students from Australia. The study was conducted in Australia comparing domestic Australian students with international students from various Asian countries.

Wan (2001), using a case study approach, reported on the learning experiences of two Chinese graduate students enrolled at universities in the United States. Wan identified "differences in culture, language, and social and political systems between China and the US as major sources for these students' positive and negative experiences" during their stay in the United States (28). The identified differences are similar to those found by Ramburuth. For example, Chinese and Asian students are comfortable with a more structured and prescriptive learning environment, whereas the Australian and American students tend to thrive on less structure and a more exploratory learning environment.

Howard (2000) emphasized the nature and quality of the cross-cultural learning experience. Experience here refers to the entire involvement of individuals engaged in their own culture and another culture that is provided by a program. Howard noted that Dewey cautioned that "experience and education cannot be directly equated to each other . . . Any experience is mis-educative that has the effect of arresting and distorting the growth and further experience" (1938, 25–26). Building on Dewey, Howard stresse that "[c]ross-cultural education [referring to the teaching and learning processes] . . . needs to provide students with the freedom to figure things out, make decisions, and develop new understandings. This freedom to struggle for meaning is not provided through contrived experiences . . . [but through authentic and natural experiences]" (1938, 25–26). If this is indeed the way to effective cross-cultural learning, Asian students have a greater burden to succeed, because Asian-Pacific cultures nurture a more prescriptive, contrived learning environment. Might Howard's study be culturally biased in that his study was based on American students going to other cultural environments for their cross-cultural learning?

A study conducted by Sikkema and Niyekawa-Howard (1987) to a great extent agrees with Adam Howard's assertions, but goes further in clarifying the function and purpose of each component of a cross-cultural service-learning program. Their study was based on experimental programs involving American and Hong Kong Chinese social work students, which included field placements in Guam, the Philippines, Hong Kong, and Hawaii. The goal of these experimental programs was to find a program design that was effective for training social workers assigned to places with culture(s) different from their own. Objectives of the year-long course included cultivating among the students the ability to adapt to and function efficiently in cross-cultural situations, helping them to become more flexible, tolerant, and creative, and develop a different perception of self and others in relation to the world. Successful students were expected to recognize cultural biases, values, and behavior; be sensitive to cultural differences, including differences in values and dealing with life situations; and be creative through discovering alternative perceptions and solutions to challenges and problems. Sikkema and Niyekawa-Howard (1987) concluded that an effective program design required that sequential learning processes start with a pre-field seminar at home, primarily aimed at cognitive learning of home and other cultures. This would be followed by a field experience of at least two months in another culture, supplemented by attendance at concurrent seminars and keeping a daily journal to yield experiential learning. Finally, participants would return home for post-field seminars and reflection to integrate the cognitive and experiential learning.

From another perspective, Merlin Wittrock (1992) developed the generative learning process, asserting that students learned best when they could form mental connections among new concepts and what they already knew. His generative learning theory applies across disciplines and learning objectives. Wittrock's major emphasis is to actively engage students in finding something within their own experiences with which they can identify or connect as the starting point of learning anything unfamiliar. Relating this theory to cross-cultural learning, the learner would develop cross-cultural understanding by beginning with a familiar behavior of his or her own culture that may be similar to another culture's behavior, and move sequentially from the familiar to the less familiar to the unfamiliar.

Although these studies are all compatible with Kolb's experiential learning theory, they suggest that attention needs to be given to preparation and orientation in the design of cross-cultural service-learning programs and to the nature of the field experience. Yamazaki and Kayes (2004), through an exhaustive review of empirically-based literature on skills/competencies that are essential to successful cross-cultural adaptation by expatriates, concluded that by practicing Kolb's experiential learning cycle, learners develop skills and behavior essential to cross-cultural adaptation. Hence, by going through the experiential learning cycle while engaged in another culture, learners have opportunities to develop critical skills to function effectively in that culture. Furthermore, because instrumentation to measure learning outcomes based on Kolb's experiential learning theory has already been developed, any cross-cultural skills acquired by applying the experiential learning cycle can be measured and documented.

Briefly, Yamazaki and Kayes (2004) noted that learners engaged in the experiential learning cycle, in another culture, had the opportunity to develop at least three skills while involved in each of its four phases:

1. in the Concrete Experience phase: interpersonal skills, including leadership, relationship and helping;
2. in the Reflective Observation phase: informational skills, including sense making, information gathering, and information analysis;
3. in the Abstract Conceptualization phase: analytical skills, including theory, quantitative analysis, and technology; and
4. in the Active Experimentation phase: action skills, including goal setting, action, and initiative.

Further, Yamazaki and Kayes adapted the "person-job congruence" model of experiential learning theory (Sims 1983) to what they call the "person-culture congruence" theory of learning. In short, person-job congruence acknowledges that a person is motivated to learn a job to ensure effectiveness on the job. Similarly, a person in another culture is motivated to learn about that culture in order to function effectively in that culture. Coupling the well-documented skills that can be developed through experiential learning, with the person-culture congruence theory, Yamazaki and Kayes created the Experiential Model of Cross-cultural Learning Skills (2004, Figure 3). This model suggests that:

- skills in building relationships and valuing people of different cultures can be developed and cultivated during the Concrete Experience phase as interpersonal skills develop;
- skills in listening, observing, and coping with ambiguity can be developed and cultivated during the Reflective Observation phase as part of informational skills development;
- skills in translating complex information can be developed and cultivated during the Abstract Conceptualization phase as part of analytical skills development; and
- skills in taking action and initiative and managing others can be developed and cultivated in the Active Experimentation phase as part of action skills development.

Effectiveness of the Chan Fellowships' Model of Cross-cultural Service-learning

Given the review of empirically-based literature on cross-cultural programs involving an experiential component, one may conclude that the Chan fellowships program, which is similar in design and learning processes, is effective in cultivating cross-cultural learning. A modified version of the Record Reflection Log (Permaul and Buhler-Miko 1977), which was developed to document individual experiential learning for academic credits, was used to test this conclusion. Instead of requiring fellows to record their learning using a record reflection log format, Chan fellows assigned to UCLA from 2004 to 2007 wrote weekly mini-papers. The mini-papers of those assigned to UCLA were reviewed by independent readers to record learning in three major areas:

1. cognitive learning about American culture, the learner's own culture, and comparative/inter-cultures of the two;
2. cross-cultural skills in relationships, analysis/empathy, adaptability/ problem solving, and initiative/taking action; and
3. discovery about self, including biases, values, and abilities.

The desired outcomes of cross-cultural learning used for this study are drawn from the Experiential Model of Cross-cultural Learning Skills (Yamazaki and Kayes 2004), simplified and covering three types of learning. The purpose is not to document individual achievement, but to determine if in fact several aspects of cultural learning occur by participating in the Chan fellowships program.

A record reflection log typically reflects a grid with two dimensions: (1) the time span of conscious discovery for a particular learning outcome, and (2) the specific learning areas, reflecting the course or program goals. Learners are asked to record their observations weekly for the duration of the academic course or program. This log reports individual learning achievement toward course objectives through self-reporting. Because the log is extracted from weekly reflection journals or mini-papers, reviewers can read the papers and check them against the logs to determine whether the self-reported learning is valid. To test the theory that the Chan fellowships program provided opportunities for cross-cultural learning, the modified record reflection log outlined the desired outcomes based on program goals, but did not take into consideration the time element. Instead, it summarized cross-cultural learning based on extractions from their weekly mini-papers.

The mini-papers were a requirement of the weekly seminar. Fellows were asked to share what they found interesting in the prior week or so, note discoveries about anything and everything, and write down any questions and concerns that arose. They were asked to document their learning, but the papers were not graded. Instead, the assignment provided opportunities for reflection and sharing personal experiences, thus minimizing any need to claim learning or share concerns that learning had not occurred.

One hundred and twenty-three mini-papers were reviewed and 492 indications of cross-cultural learning were registered, scattered among the three major areas, as summarized in Table 10.1.

The finding confirms that cross-cultural learning occurred, with cognitive learning about American culture being the most prevalent (46%). Two holidays, Halloween and Thanksgiving, fascinated all the fellows who participated. Many equated Thanksgiving with the Chinese holiday of sweeping the graves of their deceased relatives, and this was included as comparative/inter-cultural learning (12%). More subtle cultural learning included comparing rationales for career choices, observing that Americans tend to have a more community-centered orientation in choosing social, public, and educational professions, whereas Chinese people tend to be more family oriented. The least recorded learning

Table 10.1   Cross-cultural learning outcomes from review of mini papers

Learning Outcomes	# of Recording	% of Learning Outcomes
Cognitive Learning		
Own Culture	8	2%
American Culture	227	46%
Inter/Cross Culture	57	15%
Cross-cultural Skills and Competence		
Relational	25	5%
Analytical/Empathetic	73	15%
Adaptive/Problem Solving	28	6%
Initiative/Action	15	3%
Discovery about Self	59	12%
Total Number of Recorded Outcomes	492	100%
Number of Reflection Logs	123	

was in regard to the learner's own culture; however this is not a great concern because all fellows are quite knowledgeable about their own culture and would likely have few new discoveries about it.

The other less-reported learnings included those relative to relationships (5%), adaptive/problem solving (6%) and initiative/taking action (3%). These findings are disappointing, yet understandable. Certain aspects of American culture may explain the low numbers with regard to relationships. Many host families are without children or live alone, and all are working; they are busy and may have little time left for getting to know the fellow. Although the fellow may be invited to extended family events where everyone is polite and interested in the fellow, it is not really a place to develop any kind of meaningful relationship. Similarly, at internship locations, most host agencies are short-handed and they welcome the fellows as extra helping hands. Consequently, most interaction revolves around getting the work done. Again, it is difficult to establish anything more than a cordial, professional working relationship.

With reference to learning related to adaptability/problem solving and initiative/taking action, cultural differences probably represent the major obstacle to more learning. As noted by Ramburuth (2001), the learning behavior and styles of Asian students are substantially different from Australian students, which is similar to those found in the United States. For example, he notes that rote learning is common among Asians, whereas evaluative learning is preferred among Australians; Asians tend to receive information uncritically, whereas Australians tend to engage in critical thinking; and few initiatives are taken by Asian students, whereas Australian students are rewarded for independent learning and research. If the orientation of the fellows and host agency personnel were to pay more attention to cultural differences, learning might increase in these areas. On the other hand, many former fellows have reported that they are more likely to lead and take initiative at home compared to their peers who have not gone abroad. Therefore, it is possible that adaptability/problem solving and initiative/taking action skills may take longer to surface, given the differences in learning behaviors identified by Ramburuth (2001).

Conclusion

The Chan fellowships program design can be used as a model for cross-cultural service-learning programs. It can be strengthened through having been informed by other experimentation and research.

Orientation for Chan fellows needs to go beyond logistics and practical concerns. This can be achieved by combining discussions about cultural differences while addressing practicalities, thus informing fellows about the cultural assumptions that guide the host's behavior at the home or at the agency. Similarly, hosts need to become more aware of cultural differences, with emphasis given to fellows' habits based on their Chinese culture. By raising awareness for both parties, the crossing of cultures may become easier as everyone enters into the experiential phase of the program.

The W.T. Chan Fellowships Program Provisions for Essential Experiential Learning and the Experiential Model of Cross-cultural Learning Skills created by Yamazaki and Kayes should be introduced to everyone involved during on-site orientation to heighten the role each person plays in the learning process.

During the experiential phase, especially the weekly meetings, fellows need to be encouraged to move through the experiential learning cycle, beyond the concrete experience, the more familiar aspect of reflection/observation and abstraction/conceptualization, to the least familiar aspect of active experimentation.

The debriefing phase needs to be more than the fellows' presentation of project proposals and celebration. A session to review the mini-papers cumulatively and anonymously with the purpose of understanding the highs and lows of the five months' experience, and providing a chance to explore answers to learners' outstanding questions and concerns would be useful. To the extent possible, host personnel should participate along with the fellows to enable everyone to contribute to understanding and resolve questions and concerns. Through this process, everyone can learn more about each other and each other's culture, which is an important part of cross-cultural learning.

Notes

Introduction

1. For more details about Lingnan's OSL, please refer to the document "Service-Learning and Research Scheme: The Lingnan Model," published by OSL, Lingnan University. The manual is first of its kind in describing how service-learning can be implemented in the Hong Kong context.
2. Dennis Lee, Chapter 9, p. 129.
3. John H. Powers, Chapter 5, p. 81.
4. Jen-Chi Yen and Bai-Chuan Yang, Chapter 8, p. 111.
5. J. Chithra and Helen Mary Jacqueline, Chapter 4, p. 63.
6. Charn Mayot, Chapter 1, p. 20.
7. Enrique G. Orcion, Chapter 7, p. 96.
8. Jens Mueller and Dennis Lee, Chapter 6, p. 88.
9. Charn Mayot, Chapter 1, pp. 24–25.
10. Site visit and interview by the author on January 23, 2007.
11. Martin Luther King, Jr., "Letter from Birmingham Jail," April 16, 1963.
12. Kwok Hung Lai, Chapter 3, p. 58.
13. Enrique G. Oracion, Chapter 7, p. 108.
14. Charn Mayot, Chapter 1, p. 23.
15. Dennis Lee, Chapter 9, p. 137.
16. John H. Powers, Chapter 5, p. 49.
17. Enrique G. Oracion, Chapter 7, p. 99.
18. Yutaka Sato et al., Chapter 2, p. 37.
19. We borrowed the term from Enrique G. Orcion, Chapter 7, p. 92.
20. Tom Smith, as quoted by Dennis Lee in Chapter 9, p. 141.
21. Established in 2004, SLAN currently has six member schools: ICU in Japan, Silliman University in the Philippines, Lady Doak College in India, Chung Chi College at the Chinese University of Hong Kong, Seoul Women's University in South Korea, and Soochow University in Taiwan.
22. Enrique G. Oracion, Chapter 7, p. 92.

23. Enrique G. Oracion, Chapter 7, p. 99.
24. Enrique G. Oracion, Chapter 7, p. 107.
25. Kwok Hung Lai, Chapter 3, p. 57.
26. Dennis Lee, Chapter 9, p. 128.
27. Ibid.
28. Charn Mayot, Chapter 1, pp. 26–27.
29. Charn Mayot, Chapter 1, p. 24.
30. Charn Mayot, Chapter 1, p. 26.

Chapter 1

1. BG 1403 has been a requirement in undergraduate programs since the inception of the university in 1969.

Chapter 2

1. See for example: McCarthy, F., M. Murakami, T. Nishio, and K. Yamamoto (2005), "Crossing borders at home and abroad: Transformative service-learning for Japanese students," a paper presented at the 6th Annual Research in Service-Learning Conference, Portland, Oregon. See also Y. Sato, F. McCarthy, M. Murakami, and K. Yamamoto (2008), "The impact of service-learning: Reflections from ICU service-learning alumni," a paper prepared for the Service-Learning Asia Network Workshop, International Christian University, Tokyo, Japan.

Chapter 3

1. This chapter is based in part on "Integrating service education into the teachers' training curriculum," a paper presented at the 1st Asia-Pacific Regional Conference on Service Learning held in Hong Kong in May 2007. The author wants to express his sincere thanks to Professor C. C. Lam, dean of students and director of General Education of the Hong Kong Institute of Education, for his valuable comments on the original manuscript.

2. Established in 1994 upon the foundation of 65 years of teacher training by the former Colleges of Education, the Hong Kong Institute of Education (HKIEd) is the only University Grants Committee funded institution dedicated solely to the upgrading and professional development of teacher education in Hong Kong. After 10 years of intensive upgrading and continuous developments, the Institute was granted "self-accrediting" status in 2004. Currently, the Institute provides doctoral, master, and undergraduate degrees, postgraduate diplomas, certificates, and a range of in-service programs to more than 7,000 pre-service students and serving teachers. The Development Blueprint looks at how the HKIEd's unique role in teacher education can be developed and expanded over the next decade to meet the challenges of the new century through the creation of a Hong Kong University of Education.

3. Lingnan University introduces the Integrated Learning Programme (ILP) to enrich students' learning experiences, enhance their way of thinking and judgment, enable them to interact with others, inspire their creative thinking, and expand their cultural horizons. The ILP, recognized as a graduation requirement, covers the following domains: (1) civic education; (2) intellectual development; (3) physical education; (4) social and emotional development; and (5) aesthetic development. As a part of graduation requirements, all undergraduate students are required to take 75 ILP units during their three-year study.

4. The Hong Kong Baptist University Leadership Qualities Centre of the Office of Student Affairs organizes the University Life subject, which consists of co-curricular learning, a university life workshop, and mentoring. First-year students are required to attend at least eight items of learning, of which four should be a seminar. Students who have not fulfilled that requirement would be required to make up the deficiency by the end of the fourth semester of study. Should they be unable to complete it, they would not be allowed to enroll in subjects in the fifth semester, until their University Life subject deficiency has been made up.

5. As one of the mandatory graduation requirements at the Hong Kong Polytechnic University, all full-time undergraduate degree students must participate in at least one non-credit-bearing co-curricular activity. These co-curricular activities aim at rendering additional values, and helping students to broaden their horizons and inspire them to actualize all-round development outside the classroom. They can be any all-encompassing development programs offered by the SAO or support services units; and any other activities in a variety of forms that individual academic departments/schools/faculties consider essential as part of the overall requirement of general education, such as developmental programs, cultural programs, skills enhancement programs, or exchange activity/study tour. Students may opt to participate in activities that have a short duration or that last for a series of sessions, but they must fulfill the minimum attendance requirements, which may vary according to the individual program's nature. Summer attachments, work placement, internships, mentorship programs, volunteer work, community service, and work-integrated education activities forming part of the formal program curriculum are not recognized as co-curricular activities.

Chapter 9

1. All participant quotes have been translated.

2. Dan Conrad and Diane Hedin (1987, 39–45) identified three possible kinds of benefits—academic learning, personal development and program improvement to encourage youths to reflect on their service experiences; see "Learning from Service: Experience is the Best Teacher: Or is It?", Youth Service: A Guidebook for Developing and Operating Effective Programs, Independent Sector, 39–45 (Washington, DC).

3. Tom Smith is famously cited for this quote. It is also claimed to be a Chinese proverb. See http://www3.telus.net/linguisticsissues/quotes.HTM.

References

Chapter 1

American Association of Community Colleges. 1998. Service learning: Theory and practice. http//www.aacc.nche.edu.

Borzak, L. 1981. *Field Study: A Sourcebook for Experiential Learning.* Beverly Hills: Sage.

Brookfield, S. 1983. *Adult Learners, Adult Education and the Community.* New York: Teachers College Press.

Center for Business and Professional Ethics of Assumption University of Thailand. 1998. *Annual Report.* (Unpublished.)

De Corte, E. 1990. Acquiring and teaching cognitive skills: A state-of-the-art of theory and research. In P. J. D. Drenth, J. A. Sergeant, and R. J. Takens (eds.), *European Perspective in Psychology* 1, 237–263. London: John Wiley.

Editorial Board. 1999. Exposure immersion: A process to learn realties and co-existence. *Social Development* 4: 44–47.

Houle, C. 1980. *Continuing Learning in Profession.* San Francisco: Jossey-Bass.

Howard, Berry A. 1990. Service-learning in international and intercultural settings. In Jane C. Kendall (ed.), *Combining Service and Learning: A Resource Book for Community and Public Service,* Volume 1, 311–313. Raleigh, NC: National Society for Internships and Experiential Education.

Hunch, Edward A., and Shelly S. Hunch. 1998. Service-learning and forensic. *National Forensic Journal* 16 (1–2): 1–26. http://cas.bethel.edu/dept/comm/nfa/nfj.html.

Indiana Department of Service Learning Education. 1998. What is service learning? http://www.doe.in.gov/servicelearning/.

Jacoby, B. (ed.). 1996. *Service-Learning in Higher Education: Concept and Practices.* San Francisco: Jossey-Bass.

Kolb, David A. 1984. *Experiential Learning: Experience as the Source of Learning and Development.* Englewood Cliffs, NJ: Prentice Hall, Inc.

Kozenracki, Carol A. 2000. ERIC REVIEW: Service learning in the community college. *Community College Review,* Spring, 2000. http://findarticles.com/p/articles/mi_m0HCZ/is_4_27/ai_63132416/?tag=content;col1.

Kretzmann, John P., and John L. McKnight. 1993. *Building Communities from the Inside Out: A Path Toward Finding and Mobilizing a Community's Assets*. Chicago: ACTA Publications.

Mintz, Suzanne D., and Garry W. Hesser. 1996. In B. Jacoby (ed.), *Service-Learning in Higher Education: Concept and Practices*, 26–52. San Francisco: Jossey-Bass.

Rhoads, Robert A. 1998. In the service of citizenship: A case study of student involvement in community service. *The Journal of Higher Education* 69(3): 277–297.

Smith, M.W. 1994. Issue in integrating service learning into higher education curriculum. In *Effective Learning, Effective Teaching, Effective Service*. Washington DC: Youth Service America.

Stanton, T. 1990. Service learning: Groping towards a definition. In Jane C. Kendall (ed.), *Combining Service and Learning: A Resource Book for Community and Public Service*, Volume 1, 65–67. Raleigh, NC: National Society for Experiential Learning Education.

Takagi, Ronald. 1995. *Why America Dropped the Atomic Bomb*. New York: Little, Brown and Company.

Woodrow, W. 1902. Princeton in the nation's service. In *The Popular Science Monthly*, July, 269–271. http://books.google.co.th/book?id.

Chapter 2

Daigaku rankingu, Kokusai borantia [University ranking, international volunteers]. 2007. *Asahi Newspaper*, May 14, 27.

Nishio, T. 2002. The nature of ICU's service-learning curriculum. In K. Yamamoto (ed.), *Service-Learning in Asia: Creating Networks and Curricula in Higher Education*, 167–175. Tokyo: International Christian University.

Takeda, K. 2003. *Higher Education for Tomorrow: International Christian University and Postwar Japan*. Translated by J. Bayliss and S. Covell, 115. Tokyo: International Christian University Press.

Chapter 3

Advisory Committee on Teacher Education and Qualifications. 2003. *Towards a Learning Profession: The Teacher Competencies Framework and the Continuing Professional Development of Teachers*. Hong Kong SAR: Government Logistics Department.

Astin, A. W. 1993. *What Matters in College? Four Critical Years Revisited*. San Francisco: Jossey-Bass.

Astin, A. W. and L. J. Sax. 1996. *How Undergraduates Are Affected by Service Participation*. Los Angeles, CA: Higher Education Research Institute, UCLA.

Basu, S., and L. Heuser. 2003. Using service learning in death education. *Death Studies* 27: 901–927.

Boyer, E. L. 1987. *College: The Undergraduate Experience in America*. New York: Harper and Row.

Bringle, R. G., and J. A. Hatcher. 1996. Implementing service learning in higher education. *Journal of Higher Education* 67(2): 221–239.

Campbell, D. E. 2000. Social capital and service learning. *Political Science and Politics* 33: 641–645.

Chapin, J. R. 1998. Is service learning a good idea? Data from the national longitudinal study of 1988. *Social Studies* 89: 205–211.

Cleary, C., and D. E. Benson. 1998. The service integration project: Institutionalizing university service learning. *Journal of Experiential Education* 21(3): 124–129.

Education and Manpower Bureau. 2005. *The New Academic Structure for Senior Secondary Education and Higher Education: Action Plan for Investing in the Future of Hong Kong.* Hong Kong: Hong Kong SAR Government Logistics Department.

Fitzgerald, P. 1997. Service-learning and the socially responsible ethics class. *Teaching Philosophy* 20: 254–267.

Hatcher, J. A., R. G. Bringle, and R. Muthiah. 2002. Institutional strategies to involve freshmen in service. In E. Zlotkowski (ed.), *Service-learning and the First Year Experience*, 79–90. Columbia, SC: National Resource Center for the First-Year Experience and Students in Transition.

Hong Kong Institute of Education. 2006. Institutional strategies to involve Hong Kong Institute of Education. *Strategic Plan 2006–2012.* Hong Kong: The Hong Kong Institute of Education.

————. 2007. *Development Blueprint: Becoming a University of Education,* 34–35. Hong Kong: The Hong Kong Institute of Education.

Hunter, S. and R. A. Brisbin Jr. 2000. The impact of service learning on democratic and civic values. *Political Science and Politics* 33: 623–626.

Jacoby, B. 1996. Service learning in today's higher education. In B. Jacoby (ed.) *Service Learning in Higher Education: Concepts and Practices,* 3–25. San Francisco: Jossey-Bass.

Kendall, J. C., and Associates (eds.) 1996. *Combining Service and Learning: A Resource Book for Community and Public Service,* vols. 1–2. Raleigh, NC: National Society for Experiential Education.

Kezar, A., and R. A. Rhoads, 2001. The dynamic tensions and service learning in higher education: A philosophical perspective. *The Journal of Higher Education* 72: 148–171.

Kolb, D. A. 1984. *Experiential Learning: Experience as the Source of Learning and Development.* New York: Prentice-Hall.

Lai, K. H. 2000a. Teacher and student culture orientations: Implications on student services. Paper presented at the 7th Asia Pacific Student Affairs Conference, Manila.

————. 2000b. Integration of general education into the vocational training curriculum. Paper presented at the International Conference on Vocational Education and Training, IVETA Conference 2000, Hong Kong.

————. 2005. New student orientation: Tri-party collaboration experience. In Asia-Pacific Student Services Association (ed.), *A Collection of Papers by Members of the APSSA and International Guest Participants at the International Symposium on*

Student Affairs in Higher Education hosted by Huazhong University of Science and Technology, 17–23. Hong Kong: APSSA.

Lai, K. H., and T. Chan. 2004. A collaborative student affairs and department peer mentorship and service learning initiatives. In *Power of Youth: Developing Professionalism, Cooperative Learning and Social Responsibility: Proceedings of the 9th Asia Pacific Student Services Association Conference*, 181–187. Bangkok: The Commission on Higher Education and the Association of Private Higher Education Institutions of Thailand.

Lamadrid, L. 1999. Putting Descartes before the horse: Opportunities for advancing the student affairs link with academic affairs. *College Student Affairs Journal* 19(1): 24–34.

Levine, A. 1997. High education becomes a mature industry. *About Campus* 2(3): 31–32.

Mooney, L. A., and B. Edwards. 2001. Experiential learning in sociology: Service learning and other community-based learning initiatives. *Teaching Sociology* 29: 181–194.

Morgan, W., and M. Streb. 2001. Building citizenship: How student voice in service-learning develops civic values. *Social Science Quarterly* 82: 154–169.

Muller, P., and F. K. Stage. 1999. Service-learning: Exemplifying the connections between theory and practice. In F. K. Stage, L. Watson, and M. Terrell (eds.), *Enhancing Student Learning: Setting the Campus Context*, 103–122. Washington, DC: American College Personnel Association.

Pomfret, M. J., and K. H. Lai. 1999. The whole education experience. Paper presented at the Annual Conference of the International Vocational Education and Training Association (IVETA), Sydney, Australia.

———. 2000. The effects of whole educational experience on graduate employability and further study. Paper presented at the International Conference on Vocational Education and Training, IVETA Conference 2000, Hong Kong.

Radest, H. B. 1993. *Community Service: Encounter with Strangers*. Westport, CT: Praeger Publishers.

Rhoads, R. A. 1997. *Community Service and Higher Learning: Explorations of the Caring Self.* Albany: SUNY Press.

Rice, K. 1996. Strengthening service-learning through faculty and student affairs partnerships. In M. G. Ender, B. M. Kowalewski, D. A. Cotter, L. Martin, and J. DeFiore (eds.), *Service-learning and Undergraduate Sociology: Syllabi and Instructional Materials*, 14–20. Washington, DC: American Sociological Association.

Richmond, J. 2002. The University of Rhode Island's new culture for learning. In E. Zlotkowski (ed.), *Service-learning and the First Year Experience: Preparing Students for Personal Success and Civic Responsibility*, 15–26. Columbia: National Resource Center for the First-year Experience and Students in Transition, University of Carolina.

Sax, L. J., and W. A. Astin. 1997. The benefits of service: Evidence from undergraduates. *Educational Record* 78: 25–32.

Schine, J. 1995. Community service: When theory and practice meet. *Educational Researcher* 24(2): 33–35.

Stanton, T. 1990. *Integrating Public Service with Academic Study: The Faculty Role.* Providence, RI: Campus Compact.

———. 1991. Liberal arts, experiential learning and public service: Necessary ingredients for socially responsible undergraduate education. *Journal of Cooperative Education* 27(2): 55–68.

Zlotkowski, E. 1996. A new voice at the table? Linking service-learning and the academy. *Change* 28(1): 20–27.

——— (ed.). 1998. *Successful Service-Learning Programs: New Models of Excellence in Higher Education.* Bolton, MA: Anker.

———. 2005. Service learning and the first year student. In M. L. Upcraft, J. N. Gardner, and B. O. Barefoot (eds.), *Challenging and Supporting the First-year Student: A Handbook for Improving the First Year of College,* 356–370. San Francisco: Jossey-Bass.

Chapter 4

Chisholm, Linda A., *Variations in the Forms of Service-Learning.* A pamphlet distributed at a service-learning workshop in Hong Kong.

Enos, Sandra L., and Marie L. Troppe. 2000. Academic service learning: A counternormative pedagogy. *Introduction to Service-Learning Toolkit: Readings and Resources for Faculty.* Providence, RI: Campus Compact.

Jeyaraj, Nirmala. 1998. Education, context and involvement. *NCCI Journal,* December, New Delhi, 907–911.

McCarthy, Florence. *Element of a Successful Service-Learning Experience.* A pamphlet distributed in the National Conference on Service Learning at Lady Doak College.

Pushpalatha, Mercy, J. Chithra, and Helen Mary Jacqueline. 2006. Campus to community: The experience of Lady Doak College. In K. Parthasarathy (ed.), *Experiments in the Community Empowerment,* 115. Tiruchirappalli: School of Education Center for Adult, Continuing Education and Extension, Bharathidasan University, South India.

Rhoads, Robert A., and Jeffrey Howard. 1998. *Academic Service-Learning: A Pedagogy of Action and Reflection.* San Francisco: Jossey-Bass Publishers.

Chapter 6

Arney, J. 2006. Uniting community and university through service-learning. *Business Communication Quarterly* 69: 195–198.

Godfrey, P. C., L. M. Illes, and G. R. Berry. 2005. Creating breadth in business education through service-learning. *Academy of Management Learning and Education* 4: 309–323.

Holt, D. 1997. A comparative study of values among Chinese and U.S. entrepreneurs: Pragmatic convergence contrasting cultures. *Journal of Business Venturing* 12 (6): 483–505.

Kirby, D., and F. Ying. 1995. Chinese cultural values and entrepreneurship: A preliminary consideration. *Journal of Enterprising Culture* 3(3): 245–260.

Lamb, C. H., R. L. Swinth, K. L. Vinton, and J. B. Lee. 1998. Integrating service-learning into a business school curriculum. *Journal of Management* 22: 637–655.

Lawrence, P. 2005. SIFE Singapore Annual Program book. Internally published.

Liao, D., and P. Sohmen. 2001. The development of modern entrepreneurship in China. *Stanford Journal of East Asian Affairs* 1(1): 27–33.

Miller, A. 1987. New ventures: A fresh emphasis on entrepreneurial education. *Survey of Business* 23(1): 4–9.

Morton, K., and M. Troppe. 1996. From the margins to the mainstream: Campus Compact's project on integrating service with academic study. *Journal of Business Ethics* 15: 21–32.

Mueller, J., J. Thornton, R. Wyatt, and K. Gore. 2005. Bridging from university to community: An evaluation of the effect of student outreach work in communities in Australia, New Zealand, China, the United States and four other countries. Refereed conference proceedings. International Conference on Engaging Communities, Brisbane, Australia.

Park, Y. et al. 2001. An international comparative study of entrepreneurial activity and conditions: Korean case. *Journal of Small and Medium Enterprise* 23(3): 157–184.

Roces, S. 2005. SIFE Korea 2005 Program Book. Internally published.

Rose, J. M., A. M. Rose, and C. S. Norman. 2005. A service-learning course in accounting information systems. *Journal of Information Systems* 19: 145–172.

Still, K., and P. R. Clayton. 2004. Utilizing service-learning in accounting programs. *Issues in Accounting Education* 19: 469–481.

Waddock, S., and J. Post. 2000. Transforming management education: The role of service-learning. In P. C. Godfrey and E. T. Grasso (eds.), *Working for the Common Good: Concepts and Models for Service-Learning in Management,* 43–54. Washington, DC: American Association for Higher Education.

Wittmer, D. P. 2004. Business and community: Integrating service-learning in graduate business education. *Journal of Business Ethics* 51: 359–371.

Zlotkowski, E. 1998. Service and the renewal of American higher education: Two things that urgently matter. Paper presented at the Annual Meeting of the Academy of Management, San Diego, California.

Chapter 7

Abregana, B. C. 2006. Service-learning evaluation strategies and program assessment: Proposed framework. Paper presented at the Service-Learning Conference on Evaluation Strategies and Program Assessment sponsored by the Asian Christian

Higher Education Institute of the United Board for Christian Higher Education in Asia, Hong Kong.

Aronson, E., T. D. Wilson, and R. M. Akert. 1997. *Social Psychology*. Second edition. New York: Longman.

Benderly, B. L., M. F. Gallagher, and J. M. Young. 1977. *Discovering Culture: An Introduction to Anthropology*. New York: D. Van Nostrand Company.

Duke, J. T. 1983. *Issues in Sociological Theory: Another Look at the "Old Masters."* Lanham: University of America Press.

McCarthy, F. E. 2007a. Achieving multicultural symbiosis ("kyosei") through international service learning. Report of the ICU-Silliman University International Service-Learning Model Program. Tokyo: International Christian University.

———. 2007b. The theory and practice of service-learning. *Invitation to Service-Learning*. Service-Learning Studies Series No. 3, 7–15. Tokyo: International Christian University.

Milton, K. 1996. *Environmentalism and Cultural Theory*. London: Routledge.

Nishio, T. 2007. The concept and essence of service-learning: Why education in service at universities now? *Invitation to Service-Learning*. Service-Learning Studies Series No. 3, 26–27. Tokyo: International Christian University.

Oracion, E. G. 2002. An interdisciplinary approach to community-based service-learning: The program framework. *Silliman Journal* 43: 18–32.

———. 2006. Beyond the walls: Service-learning as a strategy to a socially relevant education. Powerpoint presentation. Silliman University, Dumaguete City, Philippines.

———. 2007. Impact of intercultural service-learning on students: A quantitative self-evaluation. Paper presented at the First Asia-Pacific Regional Conference on Service-Learning, Lingnan University, Hong Kong.

OSL. 2006. *Service-Learning and Research scheme: The Lingnan Model*. Hong Kong: Office of Service-Learning, Lingnan University.

Scaff, A. H. 1982. *Current Social Theory for Philippine Research*. Quezon City: New Day Publishers.

Silliman University. 2006. A report on the implementation of the Silliman University International Christian University Service-Learning Program. Dumaguete City, Philippines.

Chapter 8

Education Bureau of Miao-Li County. 2005. *The White Paper Book of Creativity Education in Miao-Li County*. Miao-Li County Government.

Gates, Bill, Nathan Myhrvold, and Peter Rinearson. 1995. *The Road Ahead*. New York: Penguin Books.

Hong, Lan, and Je-Ron Tsen. 2006. *Discover the Brain, Discover the Mind: The Symphony of the Brain and Mind*. Taipei: The Commonwealth Publishing.

Seetoo, Da-Shien. 1999. *The Management of Non-Profit Organizations.* Taipei: The Commonwealth Publishing.

Yang, De-yuan, Yu-kwi Wu, and Trua-yen Chang. 2005. The platform for sharing knowledge in creativity education of primary school: The development and practicing of KMS. Paper presented at the Conference of Internet Applications in Taiwan: The Digital System in K-12 Education, Taipei.

Chapter 9

Berry, Howard A. 1985. Experiential education: The neglected dimension of international/intercultural studies. *International Programs Quarterly* 1(3/4): 23–27.

———. 1988. Service-learning in international/ intercultural settings. *Experiential Education* 13(3): 3.

Conrad, Dan, and Diane Hedin. 1987. *Youth Service: A Guidebook for Developing and Operating Effective Programs.* Washington, DC: Independent Sector.

Hedin, D., and D. Conrad. 1980. The impact of experiential education on youth development. In Synergist (eds.), *National Center for Service-Learning* (1): 8–14.

Honnet, Ellen Porter, and Susan J. Poulsen. 1996. *Principles of Good Practice for Combining Service and Learning.* Racine, WI: The Johnson Foundation.

Kendall, Jane C., and Associates. 1990. *Combining Service and Learning: A Resource Book for Community and Public Service.* Raleigh, NC: National Society for Internships and Experiential Education.

Kolb, David A. 1984. *Experiential Learning: Experience as a Source of Learning and Development.* New Jersey: Prentice-Hall.

Stanton, Timothy K. 1988. Service-learning and leadership development: Learning to be effective while learning what to be effective about. In Jane C. Kendall and Associates (eds.), *Combining Service and Learning: A Resource Book for Community and Public Service,* 336–352. Raleigh, NC: National Society for Internships and Experiential Education.

Chapter 10

Cohen, Andrew D., R. Michael Paige, Rachel L. Shively, Holly A. Emert, and Joseph G. Hoff. 2005. *Maximizing Study Abroad through Language and Culture Strategies: Research on Students, Study Abroad Program Professional, and Language Instructors.* Center for Advanced Research on Language Acquisition, University of Minnesota. http://www.carla.umn.edu/bibliography/maxsa.htm (found under Maximizing Study Abroad Publications).

Corbaz, Phillippe. 2006. Assessing the effect of foreign language immersion programs on intercultural sensitivity. *The ACIE Newsletter,* 10(1). http://www.carla.umn.edu/immersion/acie/vol10/nov2006_research_assessing.html.

Dewey, John. 1938. *Experience and Education.* New York: Macmillan Publishing Company.

Fry, R., and D. A. Kolb. 1979. Experiential learning theory and experience in liberal arts education. *New Directions for Experiential Learning* 6: 79–92.

Genesee, Fred. 1987. *Learning through Two Languages: Studies of Immersion and Bilingual Education.* Cambridge, MA: Newbury House Publishers.

Howard, Adam. 2000. The nature of teaching and learning in cross-cultural experiential education. *National Society for Experiential Education (NSEE) Quarterly* 25(3): 33–35.

Kolb, David. 1984. *Experiential Learning: Experience as the Source of Learning and Development.* Englewood Cliffs, NJ: Prentice Hall.

National Society for Experiential Education (NSEE) Foundations Document Committee. 1998. Foundations of experiential education, December 1997. *NSEE Quarterly* 23: 3.

Permaul, Jane S., and Marina Buhler-Miko. 1977. *Cooperative Assessment of Experiential Learning Institutional Report 3: Documentation and Evaluation of Sponsored Experiential Learning.* Columbia, MD: Council Documentation for the Advancement of Experiential Learning.

Ramburuth, Prem. 2001. Cross cultural learning behaviour in higher education: Perceptions versus practice. ultiBase Articles. http://www.ultibase.rmit.edu.au/Articles/may01/ramburuth1.htm.

Sikkema, Mildred, and Agnes M. Niyekawa-Howard. 1987. *Design for Cross-Cultural Learning.* Yarmouth, ME: Intercultural Press, Inc.

Sims, R. R. 1983. Kolb's experiential learning theory: A framework for assessing person-job interaction. *Academy of Management Review* 8(3): 501–508.

Wan, Guofang. 2001. The learning experience of Chinese students in American universities: A cross-cultural perspective. *College Student Journal* 35(1): 28–34. http://www.findarticles.com/p/articles/mi_m0FCR/is_1_35/ai_74221505.

Wittrock, Merlin C. 1992. Generative learning process of the brain. *Educational Psychologist* 27(4): 531–541.

Yamazaki, Yoshitaka, and D. Christopher Kayes. 2004. An experiential approach to cross-cultural learning: A review and integration of success factors in expatriate adaptation. *Academy of Management Learning and Education* 3(4): 354–379.

Index